Making Scenes 2
Short Plays for Young Actors

A ucket of Eels by Paul Godfrey, **The Wild at Heart Club** by Jenny McLeod, **The
 notaur** by Jan Maloney, **The Bedbug** by Snoo Wilson (adapted from the play by
V dimir Mayakovsky)

 king Scenes 2 is an anthology of four short plays for young actors performed
   ss Britain and showcased at the Royal National Theatre in June and July 1995, as
pa of the BT National Connections festival

   h play is accompanied by an interview with its author by Jim Mulligan; acting
    s and exercises for young actors by Suzy Graham-Adriani, Director/Producer for
    National Connections; and the volume is introduced by Literary Consultant Nick
 r ke.

    is proud to sponsor BT National Connections, an Education Project of the Royal
    onal Theatre, providing over 4000 young people with the unique opportunity of
v king on new plays and translations specially commissioned or selected from a
g   ip of recognized playwrights.

    through projects such as these that BT is able to help bring the enjoyment and
 e efits of the arts to communities throughout the UK. Rodger Broad, BT's Head of
    porate Sponsorship said, 'It is not often that a company is offered the opportunity
    elp develop and then sponsor a project that so completely supports its own
    ctives of "adding to the quality of life in the communities in which it conducts its
    ness". In BT National Connections, we have found the perfect project to do just
     '

also available from Methuen Drama

Black Plays: Three (ed. Yvonne Brewster)
Paul Boakye, *Boy with Beer*; Fred D'Aguiar, *A Jamaican Airman Foresees His Death*;
Bonnie Greer, *Munda Negra*; Tunde Ikoli, *Scrape Off The Black*; Winsome Pinnock,
Talking in Tongues

Frontline Intelligence 2 – New Plays for the Nineties (ed. Pamela Edwardes)
Karen Hope, *Foreign Lands*; Sarah Kane, *Blasted*; David Spencer, *Hurricane Roses*; Rod
Williams, *The Life Of The World To Come*

Frontline Intelligence 3 – New Plays for the Nineties (ed. Pamela Edwardes)
David Greig, *Europe*; Judith Johnson, *Uganda*; Joe Penhall, *Some Voices*; Judy Upton,
Ashes and Sand

Gay Plays: Four (ed. Michael Wilcox)
Neil Bartlett, *A Vision of Love Revealed in Sleep*; Eric Bentley, *Round 2*; Gerald
Killingworth, *Days of Cavafy*; Joe Pintauro, *Wild Blue*

Gay Plays: Five (ed. Michael Wilcox)
Rod Dungate, *Playing by the Rules*; Noel Greig, *Plague of Innocence*; Jonathan Harvey,
Beautiful Thing; Joe Pintauro, *Snow Orchid*

Made in Scotland – An Anthology of New Scottish Plays (eds. Ian Brown and Mark
Fisher)
Mike Cullen, *The Cut*; Simon Donald, *The Life of Stuff*; Sue Glover, *Bondagers*; Duncan
McLean, *Julie Allardyce*

Plays by Women: Nine (ed. Annie Castledine)
Marieluise Fleisser, *Purgatory in Ingolstadt, Pioneers in Ingolstadt, Avant-Garde, Early
Encounter* and *I Wasn't Aware of the Explosive*; Maureen Lawrence, *Tokens of Affection*;
Sheila Yeger, *Variations on a Theme by Clara Schumann*

Plays by Women: Ten (ed. Annie Castledine)
Simone de Beauvoir, *The Woman Destroyed* (adapted by Diana Quick); Elfriede Jelinek,
What Happened After Nora Left Her Husband; Claire Luckham, *The Choice*; Phyllis Nagy,
Weldon Rising

The Methuen Audition Book for Young Actors (ed. Anne Harvey)

The Methuen Duologue Book for Young Actors (ed. Anne Harvey)

Making Scenes 2

Short Plays for Young Actors

A Bucket of Eels
Paul Godfrey

The Wild at Heart Club
Jenny McLeod

The Minotaur
Jan Maloney

The Bedbug
Snoo Wilson
(*adapted from the play by Vladimir Mayakovsky*)

Introduced by Nick Drake,
with author interviews by Jim Mulligan
and production notes by Suzy Graham-Adriani

Methuen Drama
in association with the Royal National Theatre

**Methuen New Theatrescripts
in association with the Royal National Theatre**

First published in Great Britain 1995
by Methuen Drama in association with the Royal National Theatre
an imprint of Reed Consumer Books Ltd
Michelin House, 81 Fulham Road, London SW3 6RB
and Auckland, Melbourne, Singapore and Toronto

A Bucket of Eels (complete text) first published in Great Britain 1995 by Methuen Drama
as a Methuen Modern Play

ISBN 0 413 69850 5

A CIP catalogue record for this book is available from the British Library

Front cover image courtesy of Tony Stone Images

Typeset by Wilmaset Ltd, Birkenhead, Wirral
Printed in Great Britain by Clays Ltd, St Ives plc

Contents

BT National Connections

The plays, introduced by **Nick Drake**, *the scheme's Literary Consultant*

'As the guardians of public morals warned, youngsters are enacting scenes from Quentin Tarantino's *Pulp Fiction*. However, the results were not the violence that had been predicted. Last week, there were reports of two sixteen-year-old pupils at a comprehensive near Bristol performing the opening "Pumpkin/Honey-Bunny" scenes from *Pulp Fiction* for a mock GCSE drama exam. The two dismissed classical choices such as *Twelfth Night* and *Pygmalion*, and won a borderline A grade for their performance.' *Screen*, March 1995

There are at least three points to be made from this news item; firstly, there's a hunger for new plays among young actors; secondly, there's a poverty of original plays by exceptional writers available to them; and thirdly, young people are excited by writing which is absolutely contemporary, sophisticated, and preferably heretical in its use of form and language. At the same time, playwrights – especially new playwrights – have found the opportunities for productions of their new work diminishing around the country: most theatres' repertoires are now filled largely with revivals, productions of old plays by long-dead writers, and adaptations of novels.

Suzy Graham-Adriani and the Royal National Theatre had been researching ways of answering these needs, and she and I began to discuss how to turn the situation into a creative opportunity. Put simply, we wanted to create an exciting and innovative repertoire of new plays by important playwrights for young actors to perform principally for audiences of their peers. In March 1994, with the National's backing, we began to ask playwrights whose work we admired if they would be interested in the idea; the plays would be produced not once, but many times in different venues, and with different ideas and interpretations, all around the country; there would be regional festivals at ten partnership theatres, and the whole scheme would culminate with a big festival of ten productions at the Royal National Theatre in London in June and July 1955. Thanks to generous sponsorship from BT, we were able to bring this whole concept to life in a project called 'BT National Connections'.

We explained to the writers that the plays could only be about an hour long, but that otherwise they were free to write about whatever interested them (as they absolutely ought to be), and for as big a cast as they wished. We commissioned six new plays, two translations of interesting and relatively unknown works (one of which – *The Ice Palace* – was adapted from a short Norwegian novel), and included two new plays that had already been written, but which had not had proper productions, and which were then worked on further by the writers. And I found two older, but remarkable and little-known plays; this made up a portfolio of twelve.

The writers began work in the spring of 1994, and produced first drafts that September. The first reading of these drafts was incredibly exciting; brand new work from important writers. Each play was unexpected, original and above all a work of the imagination; vivid language, big stories, fascinating characters; in each there was a various, and large-hearted sense that the world was bigger and stranger than you had thought. There were plays set in difficult urban worlds, in a clearing in a wood, in a remote village in winter; plays about love, about freedom, and above all about journeys. And however obliquely, they all discovered original theatrical ways of looking at the world *now*.

The plays were completed in November and early December 1994. We circulated descriptions of the writers and the plays to all the groups involved in the scheme, and then invited representatives of each group to come to the National for a day of workshops with the writers on their plays, led by accomplished directors of new writing. As I write this, there are one hundred and fifty productions of these plays in rehearsal in every part of the land. And the publication of the plays in these volumes means that they are now available to anyone to discover for themselves. They constitute the first plays in a new repertoire of new writing.

The Plays: Volume Two

Mayakovsky's *The Bedbug* is a prophetic, political and satirical extravaganza for a large cast; it is also a deeply pessimistic, and rather solitary, appraisal of the Soviet revolution. It opens in the turbulent early days of the Revolution; Ivan Varlet, the central character and Mayakovsky's working-class anti-hero, is marrying Elizevir Bornagin, heir to a beauty parlour, to better himself. Theirs will be a celebratory and historic Red wedding of Worker and Capital. But during the party a fire breaks out, and everyone is fried except Ivan, who is frozen in cryogenic suspension deep in the ice of the cellar. The plot leaps forward fifty years into an idealised never-never-land of a social Utopia, and Ivan is woken like the Sleeping Beauty he could never be; with his vodka habit, his swearing, and his terrible singing, he is very far indeed from an ideal specimen from this society's primitive past. Soon his antisocial habits are causing outbreaks of drunkenness, romance, and sycophantic corruption – all the very human traits for which a Utopia would have no need, and which it would strive to banish. The play satirizes a social idealism that cannot accommodate human passions and failings; and it celebrates, with delightful perversity, the survival of just those things in Ivan. Particularly apposite now, following the collapse of the Soviet Union, it is also a satire with a deadly-accurate cynicism about politics, idealism and people.

Paul Godfrey's *A Bucket of Eels* is a contemporary farce. The drama takes place on Midsummer's Eve before the end of the millennium. A series of increasingly bizarre events is unleashed when a bridegroom, Nick, runs away on the eve of his marriage to Julia. In the dark forest, Nick meets Ralph, Julia's brother. He has rejected human society, and become a wild man of the woods, running naked, killing sheep with his knife, and surviving on his wits. Nick discovers he prefers

Ralph and his pagan life to Julia and her civilised aspirations. Also discovered in the woods are April, a water-diviner and New Age mystic, Stella, a feisty woman who longs to escape a degraded urban existence, and Mrs Sparrow, a crusty and mysterious postmistress. The play dramatizes, within a classically-precise farce structure, the predicament and experience of living in the present times. It frankly and humorously shows how the need to couple, and the desire for union with another person, confront us with our own instincts, language and society.

Jan Maloney's *The Minotaur* explores the dark labyrinths of the human head and heart. Taking as its source the Greek myth of the Cretan labyrinth designed to hide the monstrous Minotaur, half-bull, half-man, at its heart, the play follows the journey of fourteen young Athenians herded aboard a boat as sacrificial victims. The group is led by the ambitious young Theseus, who is determined to kill the Minotaur, return victorious to Greece, and claim the crown. To do so he must enter the labyrinth, find the monster, kill it, and then find his way out again – something the labyrinth has been designed to prevent. He's cast himself as the heroic figure, but the play dramatises ambiguities which lie beneath the surface of things; his ambitiousness, heroism, and success depend on ruthlessness, violence, and betrayal. The Minotaur may be a monstrosity, but it is also half-human and loved by its mother and half-sister. Likewise the play's recreation of the ancient world, and of the Greek and Cretan societies, show them as places where nothing is what it seems; the world of the mind isn't balanced, rational and humane, but mysterious, sexual and unknowable.

Violence and retribution are powerful forces shaping lives and destinies in Jenny McLeod's *The Wild at Heart Club*. Angie is a stand-up comedian working at the Wild at Heart Club, but she's not at all sure that comedy is her thing, or that her life is especially funny; her partner and friend Brill writes the material, and is equally determined to get away from the town's bleak and circumscribed small world, a nineties urban labyrinth of drug-deals, dole-queues and danger in which all the characters are trapped. But the girls have an ambitious escape plan; they'll go to the Edinburgh Fringe, win a Perrier award, arrive in London, get a TV show. . . . The boys, meanwhile, are finding other ways to keep busy, wheeling and dealing, and keeping up the rituals of status and the appearances of power. But when Angie falls out of love with Howie, and in love with Risley – the older, designer-dressed, tough owner of the Club – she finds herself caught in the crossfire of rivalry and vengeance, having set off a chain of events whose consequences she cannot control.

March 1995

A Bucket of Eels

Paul Godfrey

For Polly

Every doubt that sings
All the questions that we find
Everything anyone feels
Untidy experience of things
The flickers in your mind
It's all a bucket of eels.

Characters

Mrs Sparrow, *an old postmistress*
Nick, *a trainee manager*
April, *a free spirit*
Julia, *Ralph's sister*
Ralph, *Julia's brother*
Stella, *unemployed*

The action takes place on one night in a forest in Britain, before the end of this century.

Setting

The most convincing recreation of a wood possible on stage; beech trees, plenty of undergrowth, bracken, brambles and nettles. Real turf and leaves. The fragrance of damp turf and leaf-mould brought into the theatre.

The play is set in a clearing, at least three entrances are necessary, also the facility to jump from a tree.

This version of *A Bucket of Eels* has been specially prepared for the BT National Connections festival. The complete text is also published (with *The Modern Husband*) as a Methuen Modern Play.

Act One

In the woods, dusk. **Mrs Sparrow** *and* **Nick** *talking.* **Nick** *wears a cheap suit.*

Mrs Sparrow
An undeserved present is the best.
Like this summer;
I've not worked for it.

Nick
But it's been terrible, a bad summer.

Mrs Sparrow
Today was warm.

Nick
Was that it, the summer then, one day?
Some present.

Mrs Sparrow
It was a welcome present, today.

Nick
I've worked for it you know.
Just today; one day: it's not enough.
We deserve a better present than this.

Mrs Sparrow
I'm not talking about what we deserve, but what we get.

Nick
The woods have grown so thick,
I'd like to lie down in the leaves and die.

Mrs Sparrow
And spoil your lovely suit?
Besides it could be better tomorrow.

Nick
I don't mind. I wouldn't know if I wasn't here.

Mrs Sparrow
Yes, but if you were, you'd be glad not to have missed it.

Nick
You're right. I had hoped for good weather tomorrow.

Mrs Sparrow
You get married tomorrow.

Nick
I was going to get married tomorrow.

Mrs Sparrow
You were?

Nick
I was.

Mrs Sparrow
You was?

Nick
I'm not now, not at all.

Mrs Sparrow
Oh.

Nick
And all the presents . . .

Mrs Sparrow
. . . undeserved.

Nick
It's lucky I met you, the Postmistress.
Do you think you could take a note?
It needs to get there tomorrow.

He gives her the note.

This explains that I've left and won't be back.
I'm going to spend the night to think
and in the morning I'll be gone.

Mrs Sparrow
You will wait until tomorrow, won't you?

Nick
Why?

Mrs Sparrow
Because anything could happen on the shortest night.

Nick
Before the longest day . . .

Mrs Sparrow
You're very certain.

Nick
I made up my mind.

Mrs Sparrow
What lovely writing you have.

Nick
My fountain pen. God I thought I lost it today,
I was really upset, till I found it again.

Mrs Sparrow
Nick. That's your name, isn't it?

Nick
There's no postcode on it, I'm afraid.
Perhaps you know the postcode?

Mrs Sparrow
There aren't any postcodes round here.

Nick
That's good. I like that. See you later, perhaps.

He goes.

Mrs Sparrow (*aside*)
No postcode?
No stamp!
Why should I do this?
I didn't think.
A lovelorn wood wanderer.

Enter **April**. *She has a stick.*

Mrs Sparrow
Hello.

April
Do you believe in magic?

Mrs Sparrow
When I shut my front door this evening
all the street lamps went on.

April
Often I wake up just seconds before my alarm clock goes off.

Mrs Sparrow
But I do that. It's not magic.

April
Not magic, but all magic is.

Mrs Sparrow
This 'magic' it's not so special is it?

April
I'm not going to use an alarm clock any more.

Mrs Sparrow
Rise with the sun?

April
I want to wake up in the morning on my own.

Mrs Sparrow
I've been doing it for years, and got into the habit.
Since the clock stopped in the Post Office
I simply get on with everything.
I find more happens now.

April
Do you grow your own food too?

Mrs Sparrow
I don't have need of anything.

April
Self-sufficient then?

Mrs Sparrow
No, I have many friends.

April
I have these four-leafed clovers.

April *produces a leaf and shows it to* **Mrs Sparrow**.

Mrs Sparrow
Are you expecting something to happen?

April
Anything.

Mrs Sparrow
And the stick?

April
That's something else.

Mrs Sparrow
Are you lost?

April
I'm glad you've talked to me.

It's what I like about it here:
people are not strangers to each other.

Mrs Sparrow
But I don't know you!

Enter **Julia**. *She holds up an apple.*

Julia
Look what someone gave me?

April
An apple.

Julia
My best wedding present.

Mrs Sparrow
Then I should eat it if I were you.

Julia
It's far too nice to eat.
But what else can a woman do with an apple?

April
You could plant it somewhere.

Mrs Sparrow
Julia this is. . . ?

April
April.

Julia
I'll call my first child April!

April
Why not May or June?

Mrs Sparrow
If it is a boy you can call him Augustus.

April
Gus!

Julia
It's all right.
I plan to have lots of children.

April
I plan to search further.
Take advantage of the light.

Mrs Sparrow
Good luck.

April *goes.*

Mrs Sparrow
So it's your big day tomorrow:
Tell me about the wedding, is it all planned?

Julia
We start with the cake
and there are fireworks for afterwards.

Mrs Sparrow
Do you trust him? Nick.

Julia
You have to love people unconditionally.
Trust them even to let you down occasionally.
Tomorrow, I've dreamed of it for months.
Tonight, it's as if I could embrace the air itself.

Mrs Sparrow
I remember when you couldn't come out into these woods,
not for stepping on them.

Julia
I wish my brother would come back.

Mrs Sparrow
Ralph, is he not coming for tomorrow?

Julia
It's a long training course, and very strict.

Mrs Sparrow
I can't remember where he is.

Julia
Too far to travel for one day.

Mrs Sparrow
And Nick?

Julia
Out on his stag night.

Mrs Sparrow
It's years since there's been one here.

Julia
I thought I heard something in the bracken.
You've not seen anything.

Mrs Sparrow
It's the visitor season.
I watch them, items get stolen from the Post Office.

Julia
I wonder what it was I heard.

Ralph *jumps naked from a tree.*

Ralph
Me Ralph, you Julia!

Julia
Ralph? Ralph!
Where have you been?
Ralph.
What have you done to yourself?
Oh Ralph, this is terrible.
Thank God, you're here.

Mrs Sparrow
Who do you think you are?

Ralph
I'm the wild man of the woods!

Mrs Sparrow
Pagan!

She goes.

Julia
Ralph.
Where have you been?

Ralph
I have come through a green labyrinth.

Julia
What is it, this green labyrinth?

Ralph
I've been travelling, all over, hundreds of miles and mostly at night. Often
I've come to cities and turned from the yellow lights. Where I can I keep to
the forestry, and only cross the open land in darkness. I've kept clear of the
motorways, not following any path, except twice I came to the coast, I don't
know which, and then I followed the shore for a while. I couldn't tell you
which counties, woods, cities or seas I've seen. I determined to lose track;
perhaps I crossed my own path sometimes, even doubled up part of the
journey. It has been a green labyrinth. Come now, share it with me.

Julia
I can't Ralph, I'm getting married tomorrow.
Look this apple, it's a wedding present.

He takes it.

Don't eat it.

He eats it.

Ralph
You getting married?

Julia
Yes.

He snorts.

Julia
I hate not knowing where you are.
You could have stayed at home and signed on.
Where have you been?
I write you letters in my head.

Ralph
What do you expect, replies?

Julia
We've all lied for you, you know.
Why can't you do something for me?
Couldn't you just come to the wedding?

Ralph
Like this?

Julia
You'd need a bath.

Ralph
Why this sudden marriage interest?

Julia
Six months! The longest I've not seen you.
Everyone has to make their way in the world.

Ralph
Is he performing the service?
Our father in heaven.

Julia
Yes he is. They've been worried you know.
Can't you see why I want you there?
You've not even met my husband.

Ralph
What's he like?

Julia
Different.

Ralph
Does he know anything about me?

Julia
No, nothing, what could I say?

Ralph
Would I like him?

Julia
He and you are the most important people to me now,
that's why I want you to meet.

Ralph
He and I, eh? He, and I.
Come with me Julia.

Julia
Stop it Ralph, let go of me.
Don't look at me.
I've thought of you for months, missed you!
but at this moment I wish you'd not come back.

Ralph
I'll be off then.

Julia
I don't understand, we've not talked yet.

Ralph
We've talked enough.

Julia
What do you eat?

Ralph
I take vegetables from the fields and I killed some sheep.
Cut them up with my knife.

Julia
What are you up to? When shall I see you?

Ralph
You won't, unless you come now.

Julia
Don't say that.

Ralph
You and I, we're tied, a blood tie, the only real tie.

He kisses her.

Julia
I do want to be with you.

Ralph
You have a choice.

Julia
You're giving me a choice?

Ralph
Brother or husband?
Husband or brother?

Julia
Doesn't it look as if I've chosen,
I shall go to my wedding tomorrow,
I'll be his wife, but still your sister.
It's not a choice.

Ralph
Except now.

He makes to go.

This is the end.

Julia
No!

Ralph (*he holds out his hand*)
This is the beginning?

Julia
No!

Ralph
What then?

Julia
Just part-way.

She runs off, he sits.

Nick *enters.*

Nick
Did I hear a voice?

Ralph
There was a woman here.

Nick
Oh I know who that was.

Ralph
Who are you?

Nick
Just a visitor.

Ralph
Where are you going?

Nick
I haven't decided.
Do you live here?

Ralph
No.

Nick
Me neither.
Where do you stay?

Ralph
I just lie down in the leaves at night.

Nick
That's what I'm always saying.
What do you do?

Ralph
Each night's supper provides every day's occupation.

Nick
Like everyone else.

Ralph
There's only doing and getting, keeping on.

Nick
Do you have a sense of humour?

Ralph
Hah! That was below the belt.

Nick
It's not a question with an answer?

Ralph
Why did I start talking to you?
No chat for months and now this.

Nick
You're disturbed, upset.

Ralph
I'm not a case.

Nick
Perhaps you act more strangely than you realise.

Ralph
Everyone's more self-deceiving than they know.

Nick
Can I come with you?

Ralph
This'd not be comfortable.

Nick
It must be killing you.

Ralph
I get to look at things as they are.

Nick
Do you think we are social creatures?

Ralph
Isn't it what sets us above the apes?
Collaboration.

Nick
Perhaps we made a mistake?
Contradictions abound!
First there's our relatives, we rarely get on with them.
As soon as we are old enough, we escape.

Secondly, we expect to choose others to live with and get on with better than
the relatives we had to live with.

And the result is spending your life doing what you don't like,
for reasons you don't comprehend.

Couples; it doesn't work.
Coupling; it doesn't interest me.

Ralph
So why do people do it?
Even my sister's getting married.

Nick
People feel incomplete.
No one wants to take care of themselves;
so they make a bargain:

you take care of me, I'll take care of you.
Taking care of you, I'm taking care of me;
and it becomes: my wife before you, my husband before you
and our children before everyone.
Horrible!

Ralph
But natural.

Nick
It doesn't make for a generous world.

Ralph
You expect a generous world?

Nick
I don't know.
But to do what you do, I see that as the best challenge.

Ralph *kisses* **Nick**. *He takes* **Ralph**'s *hand*.

Ralph
Into the night then.

Exit **Ralph** *and* **Nick**.

Enter **Julia** *from elsewhere*.

Julia
Ralph?

(*Aside*.) Gone.

Act Two

Late. **Julia** *and* **Mrs Sparrow** *talking.*

Julia
I had a bath.
I didn't recognise my body in the bath.
I knew something was going to happen.
I made tea. I poured tea into the milk jug.
I knew it would be like this.

Mrs Sparrow
Tomorrow, it will be all right.

Julia
My father will regret he ever let him go outward bound.
He misses Ralph.
He says he feels outnumbered, by women, two to one.
He puts the lavatory seat up. We put it down.
He says he's losing grip.

Mrs Sparrow
So Ralph's return would even things up?

Julia
No, my departure will do that.

Mrs Sparrow
Unless Stella finds him.

Julia
I don't hold out much hope.

Mrs Sparrow
Never dismiss the kindness of strangers, even tourists.

Julia
I went to Ralph's old room, earlier.
Nick stays there tonight.
I sat at the window, curtains open
and found I was waiting, hoping he'd come.

Mrs Sparrow
Will you sleep now?

Julia
I'd like to find Nick. Wake him, should I?
Does that shock you?

Mrs Sparrow
I understand.

Julia
I'd rather not be understood, no mystery then.

Mrs Sparrow
You lied to me earlier, about Ralph.

Julia
That wasn't a lie, it was a secret.

Mrs Sparrow
Is there a distinction?

Julia
Should I tell him?
Nick.
He has to know one day.
It's an uncomfortable secret.

Mrs Sparrow
Not tonight. Let it wait.

Julia
I am so incredibly angry what can I do?

Mrs Sparrow
Let me take you back.

They go.

Enter **Nick** *and* **Stella** *from opposite directions.* **Nick** *is dirty and has lost his jacket and tie.*

Stella
Julia sent me.

Nick
Ah!

Stella
You know who that is?

Nick
Yes.

Stella
Then you're the man I'm looking for.
She sent me to look for you.

Nick
What?

Stella
Now then: she wants you to come back for tomorrow.
She wants you to understand that even after the wedding there's no reason
why you can't communicate and she asked me to emphasise that it's very
important to her that you be there.

Nick (*aside*)
My head it's a gyroscope!

Stella
I just met her and I'm only doing this as a favour because she is so upset, but
I think she will go ahead without you if necessary.

Nick
How?

Stella
What's happened to you?

Nick
I met this man in the woods, he was strange, he didn't have any shoes on; but
he's gone now. He took me all over the place, and though we walked for
hours, perhaps he led me in a circle, because I think I was here before.

Stella
Déjà vu perhaps?

Nick (*aside*)
And when you want a letter to get there it never does . . .

Stella
She was frantic.

Nick
Thank God I met you.

(*Aside.*) It's better to know . . .

Stella
She sat and brushed her lips on the back of her hand.

Nick (*aside*)
What if I had turned up after the note?
Horrible!

Stella
I've done my bit, goodbye.

Nick
Hey! Where are you off to? Can I come with you?

Ralph *enters with a lump of cake.*

Stella
Another one!

Ralph
Who wants cake?

Stella
Christmas cake in summer?

Ralph
Wedding cake!

Stella
Who's getting married?

Nick
Not me!

Stella
You stole this?

Ralph
Yes.

Nick (*aside*)
All my life is slipping away tonight . . .

Ralph
Look at the sky, it's like an aquarium or a deep swimming pool, upside down.

Nick (*aside*)
I was on the brink and now I'm falling.

Stella
So you're the strange man with no shoes on?
He told me.

Ralph
He asked to come with me.

Stella
He asked me that too.

Ralph *holds his knife to* **Nick**'s *throat.*

Ralph
I could kill you and you wouldn't know it.

Nick (*to* **Ralph**)
You have such brown eyes.

Ralph (*to* **Nick**)
Cut your wrists with a blade of grass?

Stella
Is it possible?

Ralph
A reed would be easier.

Nick
I'm snatching at water!

Ralph
It's warmer at night. You can slip beneath the surface,
lean back, lie back, let yourself down into the black water.
Would you like that?

Stella
It's not dark here is it?
I've been walking in the half light.
I expected pitch darkness.

Ralph
It's only the lights over there that make it feel dark out here.

Nick
I don't agree! It's dark here.
I've never been anywhere so fucking black!

Ralph *slaps him.*

Stella
What's wrong with him?

Ralph
He's feeling incomplete.

Nick
The grass it's heaving,
as if the soil were breathing.

Stella
You never know what you might step on out here.

Ralph
With bare feet you know where you step.

Ralph *wrestles* **Nick**'s *shoes and socks from him.*

Nick
Why are you doing this to me?

Ralph
It only takes two months for the skin to harden.

Nick
How will I manage without my shoes?

Ralph
People managed before.

Nick
No. No. No!

Stella *assists* **Ralph** *in restraining* **Nick**.

Stella
Do you know him?

Ralph
No. Do you know him?

Stella
No.

Ralph
All strangers then.

Nick
My stomach it's churning.
Eels at the root of my gut!

Stella
Would cake cheer him up?

Nick
I'll not eat what's been on the ground.

Ralph
Everything's been on the ground.

Stella
He should eat some of that cake.

They struggle to force cake into **Nick***'s mouth.*

Nick
I'll not stomach this.

He goes.

Stella
Perhaps we could have been more sympathetic?

Ralph
He got what he deserved.

Stella
Have you been Inside?

Ralph
No; outside for six months.

Stella
Do you have a Disease or something?

Ralph
No. I just eat irregularly.

Stella
Are you living on the dole too then?

Ralph
On my six wits.

Stella
How did you take to the wild life?

Ralph
I was here once.
Trees overwhelmed me.
I walked beneath them.
I went up to one, wrapped myself against it,
clasped the trunk in a great hug, gripped it between my legs,
the bark on my face.
Inside me, I had changes.
From then on, I came back often,
and walked here for miles,
naked at night.
So it became the only choice,
when events turned out as they did.

Stella
Don't ever try this in a park will you?
or you'll get arrested.

Ralph
What happened to you?

Stella
What do you do when you don't want to go home?
I walked on.

Ralph
Didn't you have friends?

Stella
You think you know someone and you don't.
You don't know anyone.
However many friends you have, it doesn't matter.

Ralph
But we hit it off instantly!

Stella
I don't have a scrap of self-pity.
I wouldn't have done this if it didn't thrill me.
It has been my most vivid year.
The most taste, the most smell, the most colours I've seen.

Ralph
Do you cry often?

Stella
No one talks you know.
People sit on transport,
faces knotted and don't speak.
I started a one-woman campaign:
spoke simply to provoke.
You should see how annoyed they get.

Ralph
But I like not-talking.

Stella
I want just to communicate.
They think you're after something.

Ralph
Let's not talk much now,
or we'll get bored with each other too quickly.
I like blackcurrants at night; after cake.
Shall we get some?

Stella
The world's out there.

Ralph
Believe me there's a world here.

Stella
Most of humanity I despise them.

Ralph
Me too!

Stella
Isn't it lucky I like you?

Ralph
It wasn't luck.

Stella
What else leads us where we go?

Ralph
Blackcurrants?

Stella
Let's go together then.

They go.

Nick *returns, searching the ground.*

Nick
They must be here somewhere.

April *enters.*

April
I am a tiger.

Nick
Where are my shoes?

April
Let's fight like tigers!

Nick
I'm looking for my shoes.

April
Don't tell me. I like it:
the Unexplained.
Perhaps you walk on hot coals?

Nick
My life it only seems like that.

April
Aren't you going to ask about me?

Nick
No. I don't care.
Not out for a walk, that's certain.
There's always more to it
than that.

April
It's true. I've come for the light.

Nick
Then you've come to the wrong place.

April
The light at dawn, at midsummer.
All sorts of things can be revealed.

Nick
I'm looking for a friend, a little bit of quiet and a true friend.

(*Aside.*) Why did he go off?

April
You can come with me.

Nick
No thanks.

April
Accept it then, there's no one else here.
You alone.

Nick
Perhaps I need a sign?

April
Fate, I believe in that.
Nothing is as random as you think.

Nick
Perhaps it's my destiny to be like this?

April
No. Unhappiness it's a vice.

Nick
I have such bad luck with people.

April
Everyone gets an even deal of luck.

Nick
How's that?

April
It's the inequality of chance.
A coin is as likely to fall heads as tails.
Yet after five hundred times heads,
it is no less likely to be tails next time.

Nick
Explain it.

April
You need to think of your own example.

Nick
Hmm! Can't think of any now.
I have to admit I am confused.

April
That's a good start.
The Unexplained, we have to look at it rationally.
I can see you appreciate what I'm talking about.
Look at you, you're very untidy.

Nick
But this is just how I am tonight; you are too.

April
It's how things are.

Nick
What 'things'?

April
These are the twin principles: the Untidy and the Unexplained.

Nick
It's a mystery to me.

April
You've got the picture.
Believe me, all over the world
people are thinking like this.
It's exciting isn't it?
Such a lot we'll never know.
Whole new fields opening up.

Nick
Fields with cows in them, that's all I know about.

April
Yes, but how do you know they're there?

Nick
Because the milk comes every morning.

April
It's a new era.
Doesn't it thrill you?

Nick
You are the most inconsistent person I've ever met.

April
I'm talking about a lot of old knowledge, dug up.

Nick
A lot of old ignorance you mean.
I may be blind but I'm walking in the dark.
I don't know where I'll get to, but I'm going.

He goes.

April (*aside*)
At least I know I'm lost.

Julia *enters.*

Julia
Nick?
I'm looking for a husband.

April
You were the woman who wanted children.

Julia
Yes.

April
There was a man here with no shoes on.

Julia
Him. What did he say?

April
He was unhappy. He was looking for a friend.

Julia
Poor Ralph. Completely alone.
I shouldn't have left him.

April
It was someone particular, but not you.
He said it was a he.

Julia (*aside*)
Strange.

(*To* **April**.)
If you meet him again tell him I forgive him completely.
Say I beg him to come back.
How I wish Nick was here, he'd find Ralph.
Where can Nick be?
I had a secret to tell him.
What shall I do?

April
A secret is something you choose not to say.
But what about the things you don't know,
that you can't choose to say?

Julia
It's the things you don't know you know
that frighten me.
You still have the stick, I see.

April
Every woman should carry a stick.
You never know what you might find.

Julia
First my brother ran away,
then my husband went missing
now I can't even find my father.
What's happened to all the men?
Why is everything suddenly in such chaos?
Or is it my imagination?

April
It always has been
and now you've come to see it.

Julia
All these disasters,
storms, fires, crises,
sometimes I think I did them,
I hear the news and I think 'What have I done?'
That's stupid isn't it?

April
No. What fascinate me are the things
you don't know you don't know.

Julia
Oh, life's too short to worry about them.

April
Exactly.

Julia
So what's the answer?

April
They are all inside you anyway!

Julia
As I suspected, my fears are rootless.
I'll take one last look round and go home.

She goes.

April (*aside*)
It's too easy to dismiss what you can't explain.

Act Three

Early. **Mrs Sparrow** *and* **April** *talking.* **Mrs Sparrow** *has the note.*

Mrs Sparrow
There are two kinds of people in this world.
Those who go to the lavatory and those that don't.
That's my opinion.

April
Not everyone admits what they can do.

Mrs Sparrow (*takes out the note*)
Mostly I'm concerned with the things I didn't do.

April
But you've obviously achieved such a lot:
the Post Office.
Think of all those millions of letters delivered.

Mrs Sparrow
Have you seen Julia?

April
She was looking for that man, the one with no shoes on.
She gave me a message. She said I was to say she begged him to come back.

Mrs Sparrow
A family reconciliation might help things.

April
She said she wanted children.
She wants to marry him.

Mrs Sparrow
Who's this? Who? Did she mention his name?

April
Ralph, that's what she called him. I'm certain of it.

Mrs Sparrow
There are some things you'd rather not know aren't there?

April
Why need she marry him, just to have children?

Mrs Sparrow
Marriage, that's an obscene idea!

April
It's not for everyone.

Mrs Sparrow
Perhaps I should go now and tell the parents?

April
Why do people blame parents when it comes to sex?

Ralph and **Stella** enter, *faces heavily smeared with blackcurrant juice.*

Ralph
Because no one can imagine their parents doing it.

Mrs Sparrow
Where did you come from?

Ralph
I was under a blackcurrant bush.

Stella
I found him.

Mrs Sparrow
I wish you'd not tried.
I wish you'd go away and not come back.

Stella
You're the ungrateful one.
Why is it people like you
always treat people like us,
like this?
No wonder he ran away.

Mrs Sparrow
I must say what I think.
This animal instinct,
you need to curb it.

Mrs Sparrow *goes.*

Stella (*to* **Ralph**)
Why did she turn on me?

Ralph
Is it my fault?

April
Everything that happens you choose it.

Stella
What did I do wrong?

April
You create your own world entirely.

Ralph
Our parents, did we choose them?

Stella
Perhaps you'll learn something from this?

Stella *breaks* **April**'s *stick*.

April
I reject your violence
because I have no doubt you have a right to feel alienated.

Ralph
Can't you allow us a bit of fun?
It's just an old stick.

Stella
What exactly are you searching for tonight?

April
A man.

Stella
I've heard this before.

Ralph
I'm a man, perhaps it was me you wanted?

April
The one who was unhappy,
have you seen him?
Julia gave me a message.
She begs him to come back.
Do you know who that is?

Stella
You too.

Ralph
It all joins up now!
Everything! It's tangled up.

April
At last! What I've been searching for.

Stella
What's going on?

Ralph
This is chaos:
EVERYTHING'S ALL MIXED UP!

April
You have said it.
The pulse of nature,
I have felt it.
Now I go.
Thank you.

April *goes.*

Ralph
I think I begin to understand something.

Ralph *picks up the stick.*

Stella
This life's untenable.
One day they'll find you
in a marsh somewhere
half-starved and dead of exposure.
Doesn't that frighten you?

Ralph
No.
What frightens me
is when a branch lashes unexpectedly
and you think there's something there.

Stella
What kind of thing?

Ralph
You know what I mean,
everyone's minds are similar in this respect:
A scaly pig-wolf thing
with serrated teeth and big claws.
It doesn't matter how educated you are,
it's still there crouching
horns pricked, eyes a-glitter, and wheezing smoke.

Stella
You are a curious lad.
Is that why you stay awake at night?
It's not the things of any other world that frighten me
but what people can do in this.
Just walking out here reminds me
of those bodies
they find in the woods.
So decayed they have to remake the faces
even to guess who they were.

Ralph
All the soil is dead people.
Everything you eat is dead people.
Everything you drink passed through dead people first.
It's what we're made of:
we are dead people.

Stella
You should never say a thing like that,
because you never know what could happen.

Ralph
What shall we do?

Stella
Let's go!

Ralph
How?

Stella
Get off. Get out. Go.
Why did anyone ever come here?
This climate it's inhuman.

Ralph
Not inhuman, merely indifferent.

Stella
What's the earliest date you can remember?

Ralph
1066.

Stella
Less than a thousand years.
History's not begun here yet.

Ralph
But I found some Roman coins.

Stella
Brought from elsewhere . . .
This is not the ancient world.

Ralph
What about the early people
who walked across the marshes of the North Sea?

Stella
They began their journey somewhere else.
It's why people can't bear immigrants like me.

They only just stopped being immigrants themselves.
What's so special about this place?
It's a big enough world.
Why spend your life in one corner?

Ralph
How do we travel over the water?
Now the Channel's not a marsh.

Stella
When I was eleven,
I climbed a runway fence,
got on a plane, ended up in Madrid.

Ralph
My sister has some plane tickets,
we could get them.

The branches lash, **Nick** *emerges. His clothes are torn.*

Nick
Ralph, at last I've found you again!

Stella
Your feet, they're bleeding!
Don't cry.
Nick, your life is it all right?

Nick
I could cut up a sheep!
I can learn to swim!
You said you stole.
I do it too, in shops.
Only small things
but you should see how excited I get.

Ralph
You rub your face in the dirt don't you?

Nick
I'm a man of the soil now.
Ralph.
Please listen.
Let me join you.

Ralph
You wouldn't last a minute out here.

Nick
It doesn't matter what you say.

I still want to do what you do.
My skin will harden too!

Nick *flings his shirt away. He begins to tear his trousers off.* **Ralph** *and* **Stella** *go to stop him. They all grapple together.*

Julia *enters.*

Julia
You. You. And You!

Nick
Ah! Ah! Ah!

Julia
I went back and you weren't there.
I came out and you're back.
And you here, with them!

Ralph
He's with me.

Stella
I found him.

Nick
Hello.

Ralph
Do you two know each other?

Julia
He's my husband.

Stella
She's his brother.

Nick *and* **Ralph**
What?

Nick
Do you two know each other?

Ralph She's my sister.   ⎫
Julia He's my brother.   ⎭

Stella
What?

Nick
What?

Julia (*to* **Nick**)
What are you doing here?
You'd better wash your feet in the bath when we get home.

Stella }
Ralph } He asked to come with me.

Ralph
You two do know each other!

Julia
Who do you think you are?

Ralph
A free man.

Julia
An outlaw!
What would happen if everyone thought like this?
Someone has to work.

Ralph
Don't work!
Millions can't be wrong.

Julia
Too many don't work, and they didn't choose.
The world doesn't run on its own.
Someone has to keep it going.
What gives you the right to behave like this?
Take what belongs to others?

Ralph
Not everything belongs to someone.

Julia
You are so green!
Everything I have, I have because I worked for it.
You have to work to achieve anything.

Ralph
Why work?

Julia
It's all we have to do. Most of us work to live.
We try to give our best in the service of others.

Ralph
Why should others want what you have to give?

Julia
I'd rather work than be unemployed.

Ralph
Then that's just vanity, and fear.

Julia
Fear and vanity?

She slaps his face.

Ralph
Yes.

Julia
What about self-esteem?

She licks her hand.

Blackcurrants!
All over your face.
There are no blackcurrants yet?
You've been home.
What have you done?
Don't you care about your mother and father?

Ralph
They are here.

Julia
No they're not, they're over there.

Ralph
They are in us.
We are them.
They are us. We are here.
I care, but I don't need to see them.

Julia
You are a selfish man.

Ralph
I am you.
You are me.
Meet you,
meeting me.

Julia
Don't make me think now.
(*Aside.*) I wanted to go to bed early.
I look forward to that, the moment I switch off.

Ralph
Listen to me. I am your redundant brother.

Julia
I'm not like you, Ralph.
I'm strange.
When it's raining I want to go indoors.
I like to read letters in the morning,
wash sweaters in the afternoon,
and cook supper in the evening.
When it's wet I prefer to be dry.
When it's cold I prefer to be warm.
None of this is as remarkable as you think.
It's what civilisation means.
Nick, shall we go home now?

Nick
No.

Julia
Why not?

Nick
I cannot do it.
I cannot give you that look.
You want a look of love.
I cannot give it.
I do not think I love you any more.
(And who's that?)

Julia
What about me?
I have it here.

Nick
If anyone is,
I am not for you.
Didn't you hear what I've been telling you?
(And why didn't you tell me about him?)
What did you expect?

Julia
Not this. Why now? Why not today?
What about tomorrow?

Nick
Today: it wasn't possible.
Tonight: it turned out this way,
and now Tomorrow: it won't happen.

Julia
You were the only person I ever chose.
You loved me?

Nick
I loved you.
I try to love you.

Julia
I don't want that. I want to be held by you.

Nick
I wish I could have loved you a bit longer.
(I wish you'd told me about him.)

Julia
The love of my life.
I had hopes.
You and I we could have had something.

Nick
We had it.
Don't be disappointed.

Julia
All my hopes have been destroyed,
how can I be disappointed?

Nick
You meet people once.
You love people once.
You lose people once.
So the next person you meet,
look them in the eye.

Julia
Was it you? Or you?
What did you do to him?

Stella
You're not going to marry your brother are you?

Julia (*to* **Ralph**)
Did you take your chance with him?

Nick
It's no one's fault.

Julia
Everything in this world is someone's fault.

Nick
Don't take the responsibility on yourself.

Julia
It's not me I blame.

Nick
We have to tolerate each other,
we are all tolerated to some degree.

Julia
Ralph. How I dislike you.
I do not love you any more.
I hate you.
I could kill you.
Kill you and be quite happy.

Ralph
Except you haven't got it in you.

Julia
I could get your father's rabbit gun and shoot you down.

Stella
How can you say that to anyone?

Julia
He's my brother.
I can say what I like to him.
I'm allowed to hate him,
if I want to.

Ralph
We used to say that to each other when we were small.

Julia
I can see you have got together,
and it's been a plot,
a filthy plot.
It seems to me there's nothing left to say.

Stella
Take care of yourself.

Exit **Julia**.

Nick (*aside*)
She deceived me!
Why am I still here?
Why did I not go?
Hope can be a bad master.

Nick *retrieves his shirt.*

Stella
Did you love her?

Nick
I think I did.

Stella
If you love someone, you know it.
And if you don't, you don't.
She does.

Nick
I've been walking around with tears in my eyes for a month,
and she didn't notice,
she was dreaming I think, stars in hers.

Ralph
She had a lucky escape from you.

Nick
Thanks Ralph, can I have my shoes back now?

Ralph
I don't know where they are.
Haven't you more important things to consider?

Nick
It's not the same any more.
You've changed.

Ralph
You're a dog.

Nick
How?

Ralph
All men are dogs,
we have thighs like dogs.

Act Four

Not yet dawn. **Nick** *is urinating.* **Julia** *enters.*

Nick
Ah!

Julia
You.

Nick
I'm sorry.

Julia
I can take anything except apology.

Nick
I had to go somewhere.

Julia
Don't lick your finger.

Nick
It was wet, I didn't think.

Julia
Couldn't you have gone earlier?

Nick
I had to go now, it's how men are.

Julia
You could have gone back.

Nick
Too late.

Julia
Is it?

Nick
Julia.
If you ever need a hand, I am still your friend.
And as far as I am concerned this stands for always.

Julia
No one has ever hurt me as much as you did.
It became that I had no words:
I could not speak.

Now I know that what you did is wrong,
but in spite of what you said I do not dislike you.

Nick
You loved me?

Julia
Yes.

Nick
Your face . . .

Julia
My face?

Nick
His face. I can see you have his face,
it looks strange on you, twisted and altered,
and your hair it's different.
What can it be like to have a brother?

Julia
You'll never know.

Nick
Yes.

Julia
Sometimes you can drink coffee
and think it tea.
Is that what happened here?

Nick
All I see now
is figures of people
before my eyes.

He kisses her.

Julia
I was askew,
but I do know what I do.

Nick *goes.*

Julia (*aside*)
He's gone,
run away,
from the wedding;
gone completely.
Who's going to cuddle me up now?

It's all I wanted
an hour ago,
and now?

Mrs Sparrow *enters*.

I never expected to be out all night.
I must look terrible.
My skin it's so flawed.
I hate it. I hate my skin.

Mrs Sparrow
You wear your doubts on your face.

Julia
Every time I look in the mirror,
it's the imperfections strike me first.

Mrs Sparrow
Better to have them on the outside,
where you can see them.

Julia
Is it?
Did you come to find me?

Mrs Sparrow
Yes.
A sister and a brother
shouldn't love each other.
I understand you. No mystery now.

Julia
Did you know we were twins?
Neither of us knows which is the twin.
We have been measured against each other,
measured ourselves against ourselves,
and we have both suffered.

Mrs Sparrow
Perhaps you should try to live with yourself?

Julia
Perhaps I will think differently,
when I get to your age.

Mrs Sparrow
At your age I was my age,
I think everyone always is.

Julia
I can see
I shall remember tonight

for the rest of my life.
These hours are etched in my mind.
I had this feeling earlier too, today.
Already it seems months ago,
now tonight has gone.

Mrs Sparrow
Did you sleep?

Julia
I couldn't sleep for long
but I had a dream.
I was being force-fed eels,
a bucket of eels inside me.

Mrs Sparrow
What can have brought this on?

Julia
Do you think I shall have a child?

Mrs Sparrow
The best you can hope for is to sleep now.

Julia
I woke to find patterns in the room,
a sharp-edged print by moonlight,
squares on me.

Mrs Sparrow
So you're feeling better?

Julia
I'm not better,
I'm just acting.

Mrs Sparrow
What now?

Julia
I want a cake.
I'm going now to get a cake.

Mrs Sparrow
What for?

Julia
To eat. I must get one to eat, for my breakfast.
I'll go alone and eat my cake.
How did you know I might be here?

Mrs Sparrow
When you get to my age you know these things.

Julia
I hope I shall.

She goes.

Mrs Sparrow *takes out the letter.*

Mrs Sparrow (*aside*)
In spite of this gentle face,
I am an old square peg.
And though I may look soft
I have hard wooden corners.
Often I like myself very little
and it doesn't matter!
Sometimes it's better to say nothing.

She rips up the letter, then goes.

Nick *comes from where he has been concealed to gather the scraps of his letter.*

Nick (*aside*)
So it never got there.
That's the Post Office!
I could've gone back, but can't now.
It's too late,
What did Julia think?
Why did she say what she did?
It's a mystery – the Unexplained.
Phew!
What an escape.

Ralph *and* **Stella** *enter.* **Ralph** *has a bag.*

Nick
I'm a free man now,
and I don't know what to do.

Stella
You've got a job.

Ralph
You've got things.
Spend your money.

Nick
I've no money.

Just thirteen letters from the bank,
unopened.

Stella
Perhaps you'd like some cake now?

Nick
I'd like to try it.
See what it tastes like.

Ralph *breaks up a dirty lump of cake.*

Ralph
Brush the mud off first!

Nick
Woops.

Ralph
You don't want to get a tapeworm do you?

Stella
Who else will eat it?
Let's finish it.
We're off now.

Ralph
And our plans don't include you.

Nick
Good luck!

He showers them with the scraps of the letter.

Stella
How did you do that?

Nick
Magic!
Will I ever see you again?

Ralph
We'll go into 'phone boxes in dark lanes.
Try directory enquiries. We'll track you.

Nick
It could take forever.

Ralph
One of these old days we'll find you.

Stella
Arrive at night!

Ralph
Steal your shoes!

Stella
Wake you up with a bucket of water!

Nick
Perhaps I should go ex-directory?

Stella
It's time you went and changed.

Nick
Everything I want to do.
When shall I do it?
It's going to be a race.
All this to do.
It fills me up.

Stella
You have your moments.

Nick
If I had a camera I'd take a picture.

Stella
Now you have a memory instead.

Ralph
I'll return, when you don't expect it.

Nick
Where could I ever find you again?

Ralph
Where the eels scutter,
Where the mud is warm,
Where the cress is thick,
Where the newts squirm,
That's where you'll find me.

Stella *gives* **Nick** *a firework from* **Ralph**'s *bag.*

Nick
Goodbye my friends.

They go. **Nick** *puts the firework in his pocket and searches for his watch.* **April** *enters.*

The pagans, they took my watch,
my beautiful gold watch,
it was a wedding present,
or perhaps I lost it?

April
They broke my stick too,
or I could help you find it.

Nick
There's enough sticks here.
I could break down a sapling.

April
No. I hate to see a tree come down.

Nick
They should chop this lot.
It would clear the view.

April *goes to wash her face in the grass where it's damp.*

What are you doing?

April
Washing my face in the dew,
on Midsummer's morn.

Nick
Watch where you do that.

April
Nothing's cleaner than the dew.

Nick
Not any more it isn't.

April
We have to live with everything that's growing around us.
You can't discard anything.

She picks up the scraps of the letter.

It all stays with us.

She hands them to him.

There's no unfinished business.
Don't you have children?

Nick
Not that anyone's told of; yet!

April
Only a man can know that.

Nick
No. Not know? Yes.

April
There was a woman,
looking for someone.
Do you know her?

Nick
Yes. Know? No.
Nothing turns out as I hoped.
Why?

April
The Unexpected; it keeps happening.
Why not just accept it all?

Nick
Because I hate it.
Because the news is always BAD!

April
Perhaps it should be a triple principle?
The Untidy, the Unexpected and the Unexplained?

Nick
I see most people as either
unhappy, unmarried or unemployed.

April
If I still had that stick I'd hit you with it.
As it is I give you this.

She takes out a clover leaf.

I shall live gleefully now
because I have had my moment of vision:
a naked man in the forest
like a revelation he appeared to me,
stepped from the trees and spoke.

She gives him the leaf.

Goodbye Ralph.

Nick
Who's Ralph?

He laughs.

April
You didn't expect to find yourself here did you?

Nick
I chose it.

April
The light will come soon, I know it.

April *goes.* **Nick** *eats the leaf.*

Nick (*aside*)
A long night for a short one.
I think Julia will be fine.
Tenacious, that's her nature.
It's the one thing that's endless.

He takes out the firework, then reads the name.

'A Mine of Serpents.'

A loud ambiguous sound: a firework or a gun fired.

What was that? A firework?
It's early to be shooting.

The sound again.

Have the pagans gone?

He listens.

It should be the low ebb of the night,
but in spite of that
I can hear the gods walking
and the years turning.

Mrs Sparrow *flies in as a bird.*

Mrs Sparrow
What can be louder than time?

It thunders.

Nick
How are you?

Mrs Sparrow
Oh, I've been dead for years.

He drops the firework.

Nick
What?

Mrs Sparrow
I've come to warn you.
The next thousand years . . .

Nick
Yes?

Mrs Sparrow
The next thousand years,
it will happen.

A lightning flash.

Nick
Oh no!
But I only wanted a better day today.

Mrs Sparrow
You don't deserve an inch,
so I give you a mile.

Nick
Two thousand years done,
and I have lived as if there was no tomorrow.
Now there is one.

Mrs Sparrow
And there's another thing: about tomorrow.

Nick
What's going to happen tomorrow?

Mrs Sparrow
Tomorrow you'll wake up
and find you're alive.
Then you'll be sorry.

She goes. It rains.

Nick (*aside*)
After tonight,
I'll not come back here,
not walk these woods again.
These feelings,
I leave them here,
tonight.
Let the ghosts walk
I'll not see them.

Today: I'll get through it.

Time to be gone
but I'll not walk now
I'll run,
and I'll be waiting
for that call.

(*To the audience.*)
If the world's too big to love one person
what can you do?

Birds sing.

He throws the scraps of the letter high into the air.

When One Moves They All Move

Paul Godfrey interviewed by Jim Mulligan

The notion of someone living in the wilderness areas of Britain, crossing from coast to coast without touching a town or city, may seem unlikely at the end of the twentieth century, but for Paul Godfrey it is not impossible. When he wrote this play in 1987, he had lived most of his life outside towns. As an eleven-year-old in Devon, he was a member of a youth theatre, and he went five nights a week for eight years. Then after college he won an Arts Council Award and spent five years in Scotland as a Director, and then a Theatre Field Officer, based in Inverness. He hitch-hiked round the Highlands and Islands, an area as big as Wales, producing and commissioning plays.

'Towards the end of my time there I realised two things: firstly, that I wanted to write plays, and secondly that I couldn't be an English playwright writing in Scotland. I moved to London and sent my first play to over 40 theatres, who rejected it. Then, to my amazement, the Royal Court, without knowing anything about me; wrote back to say they thought it was an extraordinary play. They produced it in the Theatre Upstairs in 1988, and I have been a playwright ever since.'

Paul Godfrey is reluctant to say what his play is 'about' or to discuss 'what it is saying'. He will, however, explain how he approached the play. Having spent all his life in Britain but not lived in a city, he wanted to find a way of writing about the contemporary world in a rural idiom, avoiding the common assumption that the politics of a society are only tangible in a city. A second ambition was to address the present day by writing a classical play that obeyed the three unities and had a plot that worked out.

'One of the reasons I am a playwright is because I find it difficult to make single statements about anything. I have mixed feelings about most things and I am aware of holding contradictory beliefs. In writing drama it is possible to manifest these different voices as conversations and explore areas of meaning that are complex and ambiguous. For example, I know there is no escape from civilization, so, at the centre of the play, I put the relationship between a pair of twins and I made a decision that, with these two, I would envisage the most civilized person I could imagine and the most uncivilized. The conflict between these two was a way of exploring my own attraction to both the aspirations of civilization and the desires of paganism.'

For Paul Godfrey, the elements of our culture that we label 'civilized' and 'uncivilized' are integral: neither can exist without the other. They are in opposition and in conflict, a contradiction that is reflected in the relationship between Ralph and Julia, who have a powerful emotional connection but irreconcilable views of the world. Six months before the play begins, there has been a crisis and Ralph has run away. He returns, naked from the forest. 'Naked' in the theatre is a relative notion, from scarcely dressed to totally naked. The presence of somebody naked affects the other characters. Directors and actors need to be as brave as they can in staging this.

'Much of the meaning of *A Bucket of Eels* will be defined by the presence of the people who are in it. A play should be precise but it should be like a metaphor, like a poem that is capable of being understood in different ways. There are all kinds of resonances in my play that different productions will discover. You've heard the expression "a can of worms"? "A nest of vipers"? When you spill a bucket of eels, what do you expect? While I was writing the play I went at dawn to Billingsgate Market and bought a bucket of eels, each about two feet long, you couldn't tell where one ended and another began. When one moves, they all move. They have a tenacious hold on life: they embody the sexual urge.'

Like eels in the bucket, all the characters in the play are on the move, and the climate is described by one as 'inhuman'. Paul Godfrey sees this movement and climate to be both literal and metaphorical. He sees it as contradictory that we live in a multicultural society that seems obsessed with its national identity. He also sees the notion of the nuclear family and social attitudes to work as contributing to the problems of a so-called civilized society.

'I find it pitiable how few opportunities of fulfilment many people have. When education is replaced simply by training for employment, this is degrading to the human spirit. I don't think it is evading your responsibilities to society if you choose not to work in a conventional way. What is unacceptable is to be put in a situation where the choice is work or live in sullen poverty, or where you don't even get that choice. It is tragic when people are defined solely by their functions as workers. There are many ways of participating in a society, but you have to keep body and soul together. When you look at our society, the primary bond is the couple. Couples are the link that holds everything together, and consequently all the tensions of society are visible as stresses between couples. The next step is the family with children, and the couple earn to create the livelihood for the children. The degradation of this into the current rat-race is dehumanizing and yet this appears innate to our culture.'

Paul Godfrey sees his plays as a journey for an audience. He writes credible characters and situations, but in the final scene of *A Bucket of Eels* he aspires to stretch the credulity of the audience as far as he can. Mrs Sparrow, who is at the centre of communications, who knows everything that happens, and who chooses to pass on information or withhold it, flies in as a bird. It is a magical moment.

'I want companies to resist the temptation to romanticism and to look at the reality of the situation. It is important not to judge any character but to manifest each of them with an even-handedness. And I want them to exploit the magic of the last scene so that it illuminates everything that has gone before.'

Paul Godfrey's plays include *Inventing a New Colour* (Royal Court/Royal National Theatre Studio, 1988); *Once in a While the Odd Thing Happens* (Royal

National Theatre, 1990); *The Blue Ball* (Royal National Theatre, 1995) and *Fearquest* (work in progress). His rewritings include *The Modern Husband* after Henry Fielding for ATC and *The Candidate* after Gustave Flaubert for the RSC. His libretto for *The Panic*, an opera by David Sawer, was produced by the Royal Opera House as part of the Garden Venture in 1991.

Once in a While the Odd Thing Happens, A Bucket of Eels, The Modern Husband and *The Blue Ball* are published as Methuen Modern Plays.

A Bucket of Eels

Production Notes

Setting and staging
This play calls for a convincing recreation of a wood. There should be as
much real undergrowth – bracken, nettles, turf and leaves – as possible. The
smell of damp turf, leaf-mould and decaying vegetation should be in evidence.
Consider the audience's relationship to the acting space: they might also be
'in' the wood and certainly should sense its ambience. It is possible, for
instance, to set the play in the round. Whatever choice is made, there must be
at least three exits from this clearing, enabling the actors to disappear and
reappear quickly. Also, it is necessary to conceal an actor on stage, and, at
another point, for an actor to leap down onto the stage from the branches of a
tree. Mrs Sparrow, the post mistress, flies in as a bird towards the end of the
play. The floor surface might be uneven, providing places for the actors to sit
or lounge.

Lighting will be important in creating the dappled carpet of the wood and
the night sky; also the passage of time. The entire action of the play occurs on
Midsummer's Night, from dusk to dawn the next morning.

Sound effects need to be created, including bird song, thunder and rain, plus
a 'loud ambiguous sound: a firework or a gun fired' which is repeated.

The costumes are specific – e.g. Nick is wearing a cheap suit. The play is set
some time before the end of this century. Ralph is naked and dishevelled; this
nakedness might be partly concealed by dirt and vegetation.

Casting
This is a play for a mature cast of six. Julia and Ralph are non-identical
twins. She is about to marry Nick. Five of the cast are probably of a similar
age; Mrs Sparrow is an old woman.

Questions

1. What effect has the setting of the play on the eve of Julia and Nick's
    wedding had on the action? What does it say about marriage,
    relationships and coupling?

2. What was the crisis which drove Ralph away six months before the play's
    beginning?

3. How does Ralph's nakedness and wildness alter the behaviour of the
    other characters?

4. How are the characters affected by the chaos of nature? How can this be
    achieved on stage?

5.   Who is Mrs Sparrow? Is she anything more than an old postmistress?

6.   The twins, Julia and Ralph, live civilized and pagan lives respectively. What similarities do they share?

7.   What comparisons might be drawn between *A Bucket of Eels* and *A Midsummer Night's Dream* or the Adam and Eve story?

8.   What is the significance of Mrs Sparrow's arrival on stage as a bird towards the end of the play? How might this magical event throw a light on the rest of the action?

Exercises

1.   The play presents truthful and highly individual characters in increasingly bizarre situations. As their behaviour becomes more extreme, their motivation must remain credible. Give each character a solid foundation by creating a personal history for them. Decide what is happening to them offstage as well as on. Decide when they are telling the truth to one another and when and why they are not.

2.   Mrs Sparrow is at the centre of communications and she has the power to pass on information or withhold it. Decide how the other characters affect events and what motivates them so to do.

3.   Improvise at least one scene in an actual forest clearing at night. Take time to allow your senses to take in the sounds, smells and feel of the surroundings.

4.   Discuss what the characters find out about themselves and each other during the course of the night.

Suzy Graham-Adriani
Director/Producer for BT National Connections

The Wild at Heart Club

Jenny McLeod

Scene One

A semi-lit street corner. **Angie** *and* **Risley** *come out of the shadows, adjusting their clothes and fixing themselves. He is smart in a designer suit. She grabs hold of him and kisses him.*

Angie   I love you.

He breaks from her. **Risley** *takes out a wad of money and begins to count it.*

Angie   I love you.

She puts her arms around him. **Risley** *isn't listening to her. He's wrapped up in counting his money.*

Angie   Every time I see you, you're counting money.

Risley   Yep.

Angie   Every time I'm with you, you're never listening to me.

Risley   Yep.

Angie   You love me, don't you? Don't you, Adam?

Risley   You noticed anything different about him?

She lets go of him.

Angie   Who? As if I didn't know.

Risley   Yeah! You know! Your boyfriend. That prat. Howie Navaroe. Leader of that bunch of no-hopers who think just cause they're together, it means they're man enough for me and mine. They're boys! Boys R fucking Us, that's what they are, and so long as I'm around, they always will be.

She begins to sulk.

Risley   So, you noticed anything different?

He waits for an answer that doesn't come.

Risley   I said . . .

Angie   I heard you!

Risley   Well you gonna answer me or what?

Angie   Don't call him that.

Risley   Don't call him what?

Angie   You know. You're always doing it!

Risley   What the fuck do I know?

Angie   Him! He's not my boyfriend. Alright!

Risley   (*laughing at her*) Shit!

Angie   (*hugging him again*) You're my boyfriend now!

He shoves her away.

Risley   You gonna answer me or what?

Angie   Sometimes I think he's the only reason you're with me. Sometimes I think all you want me for is to find out what he's up to. That's what I think sometimes.

Risley   I run things round here. Have done for years. I was twelve when I ran my first weed. Thirteen when I nicked my first car. Fifteen when these (*Holding up his fist.*) put a man in hospital and eighteen when they put a bastard in his grave. Howie Navaroe's a bastard. I run things round here. I'm not gonna let a piss-arse-dreamer like him get anywhere near what I've got. I'm gonna kill him!

Angie   You said you were gonna do him because of me, 'cause you loved me, not 'cause of business. Adam, you said!

Risley   You noticed anything different about him, yes or no?

Angie   Stop calling him my boyfriend.

Angrily, he grabs hold of her and shakes her up a bit.

Risley   Yes or no, you stupid cow?

Angie   Like what?

Risley   Extra money. New clothes. Anything!

She doesn't answer straight away and he shakes her up again.

Angie   No. Adam!

He lets go of her and she holds herself where he squeezed her. Then he fishes a ring out of his pocket and holds it up in front of her like a treat. Her eyes light up. She is just about to take it, but he holds it back.

Risley   He's been working my patch again. Trying to take over my business. I can smell him. There's a trail of chicken shit all down the road where he's been, I'm gonna make him eat that shit.

He drops the ring in her hand. She stares at it. She loves it. She's all over him, hugging him.

Angie   Ahh! Adam! This mean we're engaged?

Risley *has gone back to counting his money, to not listening to her. She is gushing over the ring.*

Angie   This mean you love me? Never had a proper man says he loves me before. Howie's not a proper man. He don't count. You do, don't you, Adam? You really, really do, don't you? Love me?

Risley   Just make sure . . .

Angie   You've told me a dozen times.

He's stopped counting and is looking at her. All the way through, she is totally engrossed in her ring and trying it on.

Risley   And I'll tell you a dozen more if I feel like. Now, you know what this is about? You know what we're doing? 'Cause I don't want no crap after it's done, that you didn't know. You know?

Angie   Yes!

Risley   I want to hear you say it.

Angie   You're gonna front up at the club tonight, and wind him up dead tight like. And without him catching on I'm up to anything, ever so subtle like, I'm gonna get him to meet you. 'Cause you don't reckon he'll agree to meet you, until I say, 'cause he's chicken shit.

Risley   And also?

Angie   Also what?

Risley   Why we're doing it this way?

Angie   Oh yeah, 'cause we gotta play with him. Make him think one thing, then turn the tables on him.

Risley   You gotta be a thinker in this life. You gotta be a better thinker than whoever you're up against. So I turn up, wind him up, you get him to agree, he agrees. Then what?

Angie   You kill him, and we can be together forever.

She throws herself around him.

Risley   I'm gonna kill Howie Navaroe! I want to see you keep your head. I want to know I got you here. (*He clenches his fist.*) You get your head round this and it's dead easy. It's down to balls and guts, see! When you get to my age you gotta have balls and guts. You can look at it and think there's only like five years between me and Howie Navaroe, but I got five years' more guts, and I've had five years' more ball-growing time. You gotta be big enough to see what you want and then bigger still to take it! You know what you want?

She kisses him.

Angie   I had this dream last night. That you'd come for me. I was in the middle of the show. You broke down the club door to get me. You walked in, wearing a dead smart suit – he's trying to dress like you. Doesn't suit him though. Anyway you walked in. Lifted me into your arms, kissed me, right in front of all of them, proposed and carried me off!

Risley   Bit of a cow, ain't you? Dreaming a dream like that with what we got planned. I'm gonna kill your boyfriend! Tonight! Tonight I'm gonna make him fall head-first down that tunnel and you're gonna help me.

Angie   I want somebody who's somebody now, not in twenty years when we're too old to have some fun. I want you. Shit! They'll be so dead jealous when they find out about us. All the girls fancy you, you know.

Risley   Do they?

Angie   And all of them pretend they don't.

Risley   Do they?

Angie   And all the boys pretend they don't want to be you.

Risley   Do they?

Risley *is still absorbed in his money. She reaches for him and kisses him.*

Angie   They do. But I'm the one you chose. I'm the one who's got you.

She clings to him. Hugging him. Around her back, he is counting his money.

Scene Two

The Wild at Heart Club.

A shabby, beat-up large hall. The lights are low. **Angie** *is standing on a table that elevates her above an audience of young people, all of whom are clapping enthusiastically. They are milling around her and hanging off her every word. Throughout, there is enthusiastic laughter.*

Particularly, there is **Howie**, **Sid**, **Hyper**, **Brill**, **Lewis**, **Fonzo**, **Kenny**, **Sonia** *and* **Nadine**. *The girls move through the audience with buckets, touting for money. The buckets have 'Edinburgh' written on them.*

Angie   Yeah, I'm seventeen! (*All-round clapping.*) I'm glad I'm seventeen. Who'd want to be younger? To go through those seventeen years again? Been there! Done that! Do not want to do it again! Your fist kiss! I stood there thinking. 'Why's this guy putting his spit into my freshly Mcleaned mouth?' I felt like saying, 'If I'm thirsty I've got enough for a can of coke, thank you.' Please! Please! The first time you jump from your bedroom window to go to that forbidden rave, and you realise that that is not the reason they're called flower beds. I broke my right leg. Laid there till morning, knowing if I woke my ma, she'd know what to do with the left one. The milkman found me. He looks at me. In the flower bed. Laying flat out, holding my sodding leg, in mega-pain, and he looks at me. He says, 'A note would've been enough.' (*Enthusiastic laughter and clapping.*) Spoken by Angie Saunders, words by Brill Tyler.

Angie *points over to* **Brill**. **Brill** *is shy when the applause is directed to her.*

(*pointing at* **Brill**) Yeah she's the one! She's the one who sticks that hundred-watt bulb up my arse and shoves me out here. If you don't like what I've said tonight, blame her. As you know, this is the last show at the wonderful Wild at Heart Club. (*All-round groans.*) Don't we just love the Wild at Heart Club? (*Enthusiastic clapping.*) Owned by the wonderful Mr Risley. (*All-round groans.*) No, be good. Without Mr Adam Risley, the Angie Brill show wouldn't be off to the Edinburgh Fringe Festival tomorrow. (*Enthusiastic clapping.*) Where we'll be a great hit. Win the Perrier Award, transfer to a West End venue, get signed up for our own TV show, earn a million and retire before we're thirty! (*Cheers and clapping.*)

In stroll **Tony A**, **Tony B**, **Tony C** *and* **Linda**. *As they come in,* **Linda** *flicks the lights on and any laughter soon dies as the attention is turned from* **Angie** *to them.*

Brill   Shit! What do they want?

Angie *bolts from off the table top and is quickly fronting up to* **Linda**.

Brill   We're not doing anything.

Angie   Brill!

Howie *fronts up and glares at* **Linda**.

Brill   (*to* **Linda**) Go on! Take a good look! Go back and tell him! We ain't wrecking his precious club! Tell him it's the best night this place has ever had. Tell him . . .

Angie   Brill, for Christ's sake! Will you just shut it?

Brill   Well we ain't doing anything are we?

Suddenly **Howie** *makes a grab for* **Linda**. *He gets hold of her and begins dragging her away from the three* **Tony**s. *The three* **Tony**s *struggle to get him off her, to protect her.* **Angie** *just stands there watching, full of contempt for it as he makes an arse of himself. As the three* **Tony**s *have hold of* **Howie**, **Hyper**, **Fonzo** *and* **Lewis** *step up to help him out and push the three* **Tony**s *off* **Howie**. *However, as they grab him away from them, they all lose their balance and all four of them,* **Howie**, **Fonzo**, **Hyper** *and* **Lewis**, *go over.* **Angie** *watches them, but particularly* **Howie**, *unimpressed by them.* **Howie** *drags himself to his feet totally humiliated.*

Angie   Prat!

The three **Tony**s *are highly amused and so is* **Linda**. *He glares at her, angry as hell. He's made an arse of himself and now they are all looking as* **Angie** *lays into him.*

Idiot! Chicken shit!

Howie *can do nothing but take it. The audience begins to leave.*

Brill   (*to* **Angie** *and the others*) You see? You see what happens?

Brill *runs between the disappearing audience trying to stop them going.*

Come on! The show's not over yet!

Angie   You always have to do something stupid, don't you? (*Now shoving* **Howie**.) You always do, don't you? Don't you? That's why I hate you sometimes I do. That's why I do.

Linda *is still smiling at him.* **Howie** *is still feeling an arse.*

Brill   (*to the audence*) Come on!

Brill *watches dejected and defeated, as the audience leaves.*

Angie   That's why last time they were gonna kill you, I never cared.

Howie   They weren't gonna.

Angie I never cared, 'cause you're always making an arse of yourself, making an arse of yourself and making me look stupid.

Howie They never nearly killed me!

Angie And don't you shout at me!

Howie I'm sorry, alright?

Now **Howie** *tries to take hold of* **Angie***, to hold her, to apologize, but she'll have none of him.*

Brill You try and do something round here and it always ends up the same way. (*To all of them.*) Proud of yourselves are you? 'Cause this is your fault. And if my life ends up like all the other shit lives round here, then that'll be your fault too.

Angie Brill, for God's sakes!

Brill That's our audience, Ange!

Angie So?

Brill So there goes our money!

Angie So?

Risley So don't you care or nothing?

Angie What the hell can I do about it?

Brill We ain't collected half the money, have we? We're suppose to be raising money for Edinburgh!

Angie For Christ's sakes, stop going on will you?

Brill Edinburgh, Ange! It's how we're gonna get out of the shit round here. Get the life we deserve. Ange!

Brill *is getting nothing from* **Angie***.*

You just don't care, do you? You're just like the rest of them. You don't care about anything except which gang can run the most smack without getting done. You don't care that we've been there, done that, do you? Angie, for God's sakes, *care* will you?

Angie Finished, have you?

Brill What's the point taking over Risley's club? Organizing the show? Worrying about breaking our arses when he catches us, if you don't care?

Angie I ain't gonna row with you. If you care so much, go and care some place else. (*To* **Linda***.*) Where's Risley?

Brill *picks up a couple of the collecting buckets, and goes out after the audience.*

Howie What you asking about him for?

Angie (*ignoring him*) In his car, is he?

Howie   I said what you asking about him for? I don't want you asking about that scum.

Angie   Sent you to get us out of his club, 'as he? Always doing his dirty work, aren't you Linda? You think a girl would know when a man was just using her, wouldn't you? You think a girl would know when a man was just leading her on wouldn't you. Wouldn't you? You'd know, wouldn't you, Sonia?

Sonia   Reckon.

Angie   But Miss Linda-Bra-Made-A-Brass don't, do you? Do you Linda?

Linda *never really stops smiling at either* **Howie** *or* **Angie**. *She doesn't seem bothered by anything* **Angie** *is saying.*

So! Where is he then?

Howie   Angie, I don't want you asking about him.

Again he grabs hold of **Angie**. *Again she throws him off her.*

Has he been bothering you again?

Angie   So what if he has?

Howie   I warned him what would happen if he even looks at you again . . .

Angie *doesn't want to hear any of it. But he follows her determined that she will hear it.*

Leave it! That's what you said. I could've killed him right up against that fucking wall, while he was . . .

Angie   While he was what? Go on! Just tell the whole wide world while you're at it, why don't you?

Howie *realizes everyone is looking at them.*

Howie   Ange, I'm sorry.

Angie *won't accept his apology and moves away from him, leaving him alone, feeling sorry and a fool.*

Lewis   Something we should know about Howie, mate?

Howie   Shut it!

Fonzo   He was only asking, like.

Hyper   He was only asking, like.

Howie   I said!

Angie   (*to* **Linda**) Tell Risley. If he wants us out, he's to front up, break down that door, and carry me off.

Howie   What you talking about carry you off for?

Angie   Carry me off!

Linda   Finished, have you? ' Cause I've got something to say. (*To* **Howie**.) If you're up to it. Risley wants you to meet him.

Lewis   Now we're talking!

Fonzo }
Hyper }   Now we're talking!

Linda   (*to* **Angie**) Crap like you who pretend you're one thing when you're really something else? You wanna learn to keep your trap shut till you know what's what, where you are, who you are! Risley couldn't give a toss that you're in his club. And he don't give a piss about you.

Angie   You would say that, wouldn't you?

Linda   He don't! Alright?

Sonia   Alright! So Risley don't care if we do the show in his club. We don't have to bother barricading ourselves in here. Alright!

Angie   Shut up!

Howie *doesn't know what to say. They are all looking at him.*

Linda   (*to* **Howie**) You up to it?

Lewis   Course he's up to it. We're all up to doing Adam friggin' Risley ain't we?

Fonzo }
Hyper }   We're all up to that.

Lewis   Ain't we, Howie mate?

Linda *is looking at* **Howie***, who seems to have been paralysed by his thoughts.*

Linda   Don't look like it. Wait till this gets out. Chicken shit. You won't be the big man you reckon you are Howie Navaroe.

Linda *is about to go followed by the three* **Tony***s.*

Lewis   Howie!

Angie *heads* **Linda** *off and speaks to her.* **Howie** *is watching them.*

Lewis   (*in* **Howie**'s *ear*) This ain't looking too good, Howie mate. We in or what?

Angie *turns away from* **Linda** *and looks at* **Howie**.

(*still in* **Howie**'s *ear*) A simple 'yes' is all that's needed here, Howie mate.

Linda *has stopped at the door.*

Angie   I know the man I love. I know who I am. What I want. Tell her yes. Tell her you'll meet Risley. And you'll do him.

Fonzo
Hyper } Yes!
Lewis

Linda *and the three* **Tony**'s *leave.*

Scene Three

A street. Late at night. **Howie**, **Sid**, **Hyper**, **Kenny**, **Fonzo** *and* **Lewis** *are all waiting.* **Howie** *is smart in a designer suit, not unlike* **Risley***'s.* **Kenny** *has his head in a book.*

Lewis   All we've got to do is remember why we're here.

Hyper
Fonzo }   Yeah!

Lewis   All we've got to do is remember what doing Risley will do for us around here.

Hyper
Fonzo }   Yeah!

All we've got to do is do him, and we'll run things round here.

Howie   Shut it!

Fonzo   We were only saying.

Hyper   Yeah, we were only saying, like, Howie mate.

Lewis   Howie's right. Shut it. Anyway Hyper, you wouldn't know what to say in a monastery full of dumb monks, would you?

Hyper   I would. Say a lot of interesting things I do.

Hyper *begins to laugh at himself. They all do, except* **Howie** *and* **Sid***, who are both off in their own worlds.*

Lewis   Yeah, that's why Dulux want you for their next TV ad.

All of them crack up laughing, even **Hyper***. Only* **Howie** *and* **Sid** *aren't laughing.*

Sid   (*over the laughter*) I don't reckon they're coming.

Kenny   This is what people like Risley do. You know where you're going. You think it's safe, and then suddenly, there you are.

Hyper   Where like?

Kenny   There! Anywhere! But always a place you don't want to be. And always in a hole full of shit.

Sid   They could be at the club. Causing trouble on the girls. Laughing at us, waiting here, like idiots.

Lewis   He could be right.

Sid   Finally! Someone listens, someone agrees with me.

Lewis   I mean, they're cowards, aren't they? I saw that Tony C in a dress the other day.

Hyper   Jeeezus! Out like was he?

Lewis   I'm not gonna be inside with Tony C wearing a dress, am I? Brazen he was!

Hyper   Yeah?

Lewis   Dead tight it was.

Hyper   Yeah?

Lewis   Yeah.

Hyper   What colour like?

Lewis   Same colour as that lipstick I kissed off Julia Beckett last night.

Fonzo   You did Julia Beckett last night?

Lewis   Ask me again.

Fonzo   You did Julia Beckett?

Lewis   Fonzo, I did do Julia Beckett last night!

Hyper   Jeezus!

Lewis   Right up against Patel's chip shop window.

Fonzo   I've always fancied Julia Beckett.

Hyper   You fancy every girl, you do.

Lewis   Nearly broke the bleedin' shop window we did.

Fonzo   Jeezus!

Lewis   Only cost me a bag of chips too.

Fonzo   What's the cheapest you ever spent for it, Howie?

Howie   A drag on her cigarette.

Lewis
Hyper } Wowhoow!
Fonzo

Hyper   Who was it then?

Howie   Horizontal Sonia. Only she wasn't, like

Laughter. Proud, slapping-on-the-back laughter.

Hyper   Shit! I fancy her.

Howie   She just kept saying, 'I'm coming, I'm coming with you.'

Hyper   Coming where, like?

Howie   In my red Mercedes convertible Hyper! (*They laugh at* **Hyper**, *who doesn't understand, but laughs anyway.*) Black leather seats, alloy wheels, CD player, car phone, Ange next to me, glove compartment stuffed full of Rizzla, back seat full of Cadbury's Flake, blue sky over head. And plenty of respect!

*For a moment they all savour **Howie**'s dream.*

Sid   (*up in **Lewis**'s face*) Liar! Liar! Liar!

Hyper
Lewis   } Whoowhooo!
Fonzo

Sid   That's all you do. To get yourself noticed. Tell lies. You never saw Tony C in any dress.

Lewis   I saw him! And you know what he said? He said tell Sidney not to wear his pink, 'cause as you can see, I'm wearing mine!

They all crack up laughing.

Sid   Piss off!

Howie   Go easy, Sid.

Sid   And you can piss off as well.

Howie   I'm your best mate. You can't tell me to piss off.

Sid   Piss off!

*More laughter. **Sid** picks up a rock and makes to go at **Lewis** with it. But **Hyper** and **Fonzo** grab him and stop him. The laughter stops.*

Lewis   Yeah! Yeah! Come on then! Come on then!

*Sid is being held. **Howie** takes the rock from his hand.*

Lewis   Come on, you wanker!

Howie   (*to **Lewis***) Shut it!

Lewis   He's useless! Useless! You're a useless prat, Sidney Weeks.

Howie   We sat next to each other in school, he did my homework and I did his screwing. He's my mate. You saying I'm a useless prat too?

Lewis   No, Howie mate.

Howie   Then don't say he is. (*To **Hyper** and **Fonzo**.*) Let go of him.

*They let go of him. **Sid** drags himself away and marches off into the dark.*

Howie   Sidney! Where you going? Sidney!

Sid has gone.

Hyper   Now look what you done.

Fonzo   It was only a laugh.

Hyper   Sid don't get jokes.

Lewis   Bit like him and the girls really.

They all crack up laughing. All except **Howie**, *who has gone into his own world. They all stop laughing when they see him.*

Lewis Howie, what did you mean when you told Ange 'I could've done him up against the wall?'

Fonzo Risley ain't done your Ange, has he, Howie mate?

Lewis 'Cause if he has, you know we'll kill him.

Hyper You know we will.

Fonzo
Lewis } You know we will.

Howie He tried! She said no! She said no. Alright?

They all stare at him, feeling sorry for him. Something alerts **Lewis**.

Lewis You hear that?

They all listen. A shuffling sound is heard. They are all alert. **Lewis** *pulls a club of wood from under his jacket. They all do the same.* **Kenny** *puts his book away, but has no weapon.*

Lewis This is it, lads!

They look around. Trying to cover all angles. Not knowing which way the attack will come. They form themselves into a circle looking out. Alert, ready, they wait. It goes quiet.

Lewis See anything?

Fonzo Nothing.

Lewis Hear anything?

Hyper Nothing.

Lewis Nothing!

They wait. It's quiet.

Lewis (*shouting*) Come on, you bastards!

Out of nowhere something is shoved at them. At **Lewis**.

Ah!

Shocked, he steps back and whatever it is, drops to the ground in a heap.

Shit!

On the ground, they all stare down at a tied-up, trussed-up, beaten, gagged and bleeding body. It's **Sid**.

Hyper Jeezus!

Fonzo He ain't dead is he?

Howie *is kneeling over* **Sid**, *taking the gag off.* **Sid** *won't answer.* **Howie** *stands up from him.*

Howie   Get that crap off him.

Lewis, **Hyper** and **Fonzo** *set about undoing the ropes. That done, they all hover over him, peering down at him.*

Kenny   Get back. Get back.

Kenny *pushes them back. They all wait for* **Sid** *to speak, but he doesn't.*

Fonzo   (*Pointing at* **Sid**) Eeeeee! Look! He's pissed himself!

Sid *begins to cry.* **Howie** *moves away, the others take his lead. All of them embrarrassed by* **Sid**'s *tears. All of them except* **Kenny**, *who stays close to him.*

Howie   I'm gonna kill him. I'm gonna fucking kill him. He's mouthed me off. He's done my girlfriend, he's done my best mate. Not his business. Not his money. Not anything, but him.

Sid *struggles to his feet.* **Kenny** *moves to help him, but he doesn't want any help.*

Sid   Get off! Just get off me!

Sid *walks away. He stands alone. His sobs are clearly heard. All of them are too embarrassed to hear them.*

Scene Four

The Wild at Heart Club.

It's the middle of the night/early hours of the morning. It's quiet, except **Sonia**, *in her sleeping bag, is snoring loudly.* **Nadine** *is trying to pull her by the arm to roll her off her back and onto her side.* **Nadine** *is having great difficulty.*

Brill *is counting the money in the buckets.* **Angie** *is awake and staring into space.*

In front of the door, a table forms a barricade and there are bits of camping gear around.

Brill   Twenty-eight pounds, fifty-two pence.

Nadine   She told me, she slept through her sister giving birth. It was just them in the house. She went to sleep. Woke up, and her sister had this new person for breakfast.

Brill   To eat like?

Nadine   (*still struggling with* **Sonia**) Shit, she's heavy!

Brill   Nadine, you listening to me?

Nadine   I can't imagine it. Waking up and your life changing like that.

Brill   (*up in* **Nadine**'s *face*) Twenty-eight pounds! Fifty-two friggin' pence.

Finally rolling **Sonia**.

Nadine   Well! It's not my fault is it? It's not my fault that lot turned up is it?

Sonia *stops snoring.*

Brill   I never said it was, did I? Did I?

Nadine   I thought it'd be dead good staying here. A couple of nights, camping out like. Pretending we were. Just us girls. Before every single thing in our lives changed forever. If I'd known you were gonna be so narky, Brill Tyler, I never would've agreed to help you and Ange out.

Brill   All I'm saying is we took over this place for nothing. We should've made hundreds, and we made twenty-eight pounds and fifty-two friggin' pence. How far me and Angie gonna get on that?

Nadine   Even if things never got wrecked, you wouldn't have made hundreds.

Brill   We would.

Nadine *looks sceptical.*

Brill   We would've!

Nadine *goes over to the kettle and starts to make tea.*

Brill   Tomorrow me and Ange'll be in Edinburgh. We'll be the ones waking up to find our lives changed, 'cause we're brave enough to.

Nadine   What's that mean?

Brill   Whatever you want it to mean, Nadine!

Nadine   I don't intend staying at that nursing-home forever, you know?

Brill   Did I mention nursing-home?

Nadine   But I know what you mean, Brill Tyler. Writing a few jokes? Telling them to a bunch of strangers? That ain't exactly normal work is it?

Brill   And sticking your hand up someone's arse is?

Nadine   *Once* I told you I did that! Once! And you're always on about it now, aren't you?

Angie *throws her head out of her sleeping bag and glares at them.*

Angie   Shut up!

Angie *goes back under her sleeping bag.*

Brill   What's the matter with her, then?

Nadine   Don't tell me you ain't noticed? Been weird for weeks. Sonia's been wondering.

Brill   Wondering what?

Nadine   If she might be pregnant, like.

Brill   If she was pregnant, I would know.

Nadine   Yeah! Sure!

Brill   I'm her best mate, aren't I? Course I'd know.

Nadine   How would you? Unless she told you, like?

Brill   And she would. If she was!

Angie *again throws her head from under the sleeping bag and looks at the two of them.*

Angie   I haven't been weird for ages, alright? I'm not pregnant, alright? And if I was, would it be any business of yours?

Angie *gets up.*

Nadine   I never said you were pregnant. I never even thought it. It was Sonia who said you were.

Angie   What time is it?

Brill   Half-hour more than the last time you asked.

Angie   (*to* **Brill**) Just 'cause you don't care about Lewis no more. Howie's out there!

Brill   You sent him after that nutter, didn't you?

Angie   Every time I do something, I have to explain it to you, don't I? And you know why?

Brill   No I don't Ange. Go on, tell us then.

Angie   Cause you've never had a man worship you, that's why.

Brill *is laughing at her, but* **Angie** *is being totally sincere.*

Brill   And Howie Navaroe worships you, does he?

Angie   So what if he does? So what if someone else does?

Nadine   Someone like who?

Angie   (*to* **Brill**) Wouldn't be any business of yours, would it?

Nadine   Ahhh! You got a new man! You got a new man? (*To* **Brill**.) You never told me she had a new man? (*To* **Angie**.) Who?

Angie   If I have, I ain't telling you.

Nadine   Go on, Ange. Go on. I won't say nothing if you don't want me to. Who am I gonna say anything to anyway?

Brill, *arms folded high on her chest, is glaring at* **Angie**. **Angie** *is wallowing in the attention from* **Nadine** *and playing it up for all it's worth.*

Nadine   (*to* **Brill**) Go on. Tell us.

Angie   Alright! Alright!

Angie *pulls a chain that's around her neck from beneath her top and shows it off, dead proud. Hanging from the chain is the ring* **Risley** *gave her.* **Nadine** *is mesmerized by it.* **Brill** *remains glaring at* **Angie**.

Nadine   Ahhhhhh!

Nadine *rushs forward to look at it and touch it and drool over it.*

Nadine   Shit! Ange!

Angie   Yeah!

Nadine   You lucky bitch! It's beautiful! Brill, ain't it beautiful?

Angie   Costs loads too.

Nadine   Shit!

Angie   We were down town last week. We saw it in a shop window. We saw it at exactly the same time. I looked at him, he looked at me. Nadine, we didn't even have to speak.

Nadine   Shit! That's love, that is. That's real love!

Angie   That's how it is with me and him. We just know what the other one's thinking without even talking. We bought it then and there and he put it on my finger and kissed it. Nadine, it cost loads!

Nadine   Shit!

Angie   He's loaded. He don't care. So long as I'm happy, like. I'm not wearing it properly yet, 'cause he thinks we should wait to tell Howie.

Nadine   Do I know him?

Angie   We agreed we'd tell Howie and then everyone else. It's only fair.

Nadine   You done it with him, ain't you? I can tell. What's he like?

Angie   I ain't telling you, am I?

Nadine   Ahhh! Go on!

Angie *puts her arm around* **Nadine**'s *neck and whispers something to her. They both crack up laughing.*

Brill   You're just a stupid cow, aren't you?

Angie *and* **Nadine** *stop laughing.* **Angie** *and* **Brill** *glare at each other.*

Angie   Might a known you'd be happy for me.

Brill   What about Edinburgh? What about what we said?

Angie   Just 'cause I'm in love, it don't mean no to Edinburgh, does it?

Nadine   It don't mean that, Brill.

Brill   (*mocking* **Angie**) 'It don't mean no to Edinburgh' I know her. Every time she falls in love, it's like she stops breathing or something. It's like nothing else in the whole wide world matters but some man and what he wants.

Angie   Finished slagging me off, have you?

Brill   We're going to the Edinburgh Festival! Get away from falling in love with no-hopers, having their kids and living off the Social. Win the Perrier. That's what we said, Angela.

Angie   I know what we said.

Brill   It's what we said we'd do.

Angie   I know!

Brill   And you go and fall in friggin' love?

Angie *isn't listening.* **Brill** *chases her with it.*

Brill   Ange! Only dead interesting people go to the Edinburgh Festival.
Dead interesting people, wearing dead interesting clothes, hanging out at
dead interesting places. We're suppose to meet them, be one of them, at the
centre of the universe that is Edinburgh. You said!

Angie *stares her out. There's a loud banging on the door.* **Sonia** *rolls over. The banging
comes again.*

Sonia   Shit! Who's that?

Brill *and* **Nadine** *look worried.* **Angie** *almost has a smile on her face.*

Angie   Risley!

The banging comes again.

Nadine   Shouldn't we let him in? Or something?

Angie   No!

The banging comes again.

Nadine   If we don't let him in and he breaks down his own club door, he's
gonna kill us.

Brill   She's right.

Angie   He won't. Let him break it down.

More banging.

Sonia   And I'd just gone off!

Sonia *is struggling with her sleeping bag. The others are alert and looking at the door,
waiting for the banging to stop.*

Sonia   Just when I was having the weirdest dream of my life!

Sonia *struggles upright in her sleeping bag. The banging stops.*

Nadine   Risley wouldn't knock!

Angie   Not exactly a knock.

Sonia *is getting out of her sleeping bag. The others all wait for the banging to start
again.*

Sonia   I was on stage, see. At Wembley. Singing a Madonna song. There
was this great big audience. And they were all men. All there for me! As I
was coming to the end of my set, 'cause that's what they're called, aren't they?
As I was coming to the end of my set, the crowd split in two. One lot turned
red, one lot turned blue. A whistle went and they started to play football.

Thousands on one team, thousands on the other. And this is the weird bit, I'd become their audience!

Still no one is listening to her.

Sonia   You start off as one thing and end up another! Great, innit?

Nadine *has her ear to the door, but she can't hear anything.*

Angie   Sonia shut your trap! (*To* **Nadine**.) He's gone, hasn't he? Hasn't he, Nadine?

Sonia   I was only saying, like.

Angie   Risley's gone, hasn't he?

Nadine   I don't know, do I? I can't hear anything.

Angie *shoves* **Nadine** *out the way and listens herself. There is a single bang, which frightens* **Angie**, *but then has her smiling.*

Lewis   (*off*) Brill, open the door. It's me, Lewis!

Whatever smile **Angie** *had on her face, disappears. She steps back without attempting to open the door.*

Sonia   Couldn't be anyone nice, could it? What's he want?

Brill   Permission to take his last friggin' breath if I have anything to do with it.

Nadine   I bet he's come perving, the dirty bastard.

Brill, **Nadine** and **Sonia** *are laughing, as they begin to move the table.*

Sonia   Trying to catch us in our nighties or something.

Angie   Better than without, ah Sonia? You cheap slag.

The three of them stop with the table and look at **Angie**.

Sonia   Ah! What have I done?

Angie   You're a slag. Whatever man any of us are with, you have to go offering yourself up like you'd die if you didn't.

Brill   Angie!

Angie   (*to* **Brill**) You'd still be with Lewis if she didn't jump him. Only saying what everyone's been thinking.

Sonia   That what everyone's been thinking?

Angie   And don't come it.

Sonia   It's not like I forced him or anything, it's not like I was the one who actually split you and him up or anything.

Angie   No, you didn't!

Brill   Sonia, I don't care about Lewis. Alright? (*to* **Angie**.) Alright?

Nadine *and* **Brill** *go back to moving the table from the door.* **Sonia** *sulks for a bit.* **Angie** *looks miserable.*

Nadine   Shit! You know what this means don't you? They've managed to do Risley.

Angie *looks worried.*

The table moves. The door opens and **Howie** *is the first to come through. He has a dirty great smile on his face, grinning at everyone. In front of him, with a gag over her mouth and her arms tied behind her back, he marches in an angry and embarrassed* **Linda**. *The girls can't believe their eyes.*

Howie   Hiya, Ange.

In comes **Kenny**, *who is helping* **Sid**, *who looks a state. Then in struggle* **Hyper**, **Fonzo** *and* **Lewis**. *The three of them are carrying* **Risley** *by the feet and arms.* **Risley** *is bound, gagged, beaten and powerless.* **Brill**, **Nadine** *and* **Sonia** *stand flabbergasted and staring at the state of* **Risley**.

Meanwhile, **Angie** *is moving over to where they are holding* **Risley**. *Now she stands absolutely stunned at the state of him. The position he's in, slung unceremoniously between* **Hyper**, **Fonzo** *and* **Lewis**.

Sonia   Uhuhuhuhuh!

Brill   Jesus Christ!

Sonia   Almighty!

Nadine   In heaven!

Sonia   God!

At some point, **Angie** *turns her back on* **Risley**, *unable to look at him any longer.*

Howie   (*still with that grin*) We got him then. We found him trying to break in. Didn't we, lads?

Hyper
Fonzo   } Yeah, yeah, we did.
Lewis

Howie   We waited for him, but he didn't show. So we came to see you were alright, and we find him breaking in. Didn't we, lads?

Hyper
Fonzo } Yeah.
Lewis

Howie Axes, crowbars, axes . . . And then round the corner, on her own. We find Miss Linda-Bra-Made-A-Brass, sitting in his car waiting for him. Legs open. On her own. No sign a the three Tonys or their pink frocks. (*Grabbing hold of* **Linda**.) We know about them pink frocks.

The lads, except **Sid** *and* **Kenny**, *let out a nervous false laugh.*

Linda *struggles to say something, but whatever it is can't be understood under the gag.*

The girls continue to stare at **Risley**. *All of them unable to speak.*

Brill *is down on her knees, looking closely, still shocked, at the state of* **Risley**.

Howie (*to* **Brill**) What you looking at?

Kenny I told you we shouldn't have done it.

Howie (*to* **Brill**) What you looking at?

Kenny We shouldn't a done it!

Howie Done what? We hardly touched him. (*To* **Brill**.) I said, what you looking at?

Brill What you gone and done now.

Howie (*grinning*) Him! We gone and done him.

Hyper
Fonzo } We gone and done him.
Lewis

Lewis Good and proper, the bastard.

Howie Ain't such a big dick now are you, Risley? Ain't such a big dick going round slagging me and my mates off, are you Risley? To be putting your dirty hands on things that don't belong to you.

Brill What have you gone and done?

Howie What does it look like?

Brill He should be in hospital. You called an ambulance?

Kenny *immediately moves to the door to go and phone for the ambulance but* **Howie** *stops him.*

Brill (*to* **Kenny**) Go on!

But **Howie** *won't let him go. They all stare at* **Howie** *except* **Angie** *who is still turned away, still in her own world. All of them pleading with* **Howie** *to let* **Kenny** *go and call.*

Howie   What you all looking at me like that for? (*To the girls.*) You want to get to Edinburgh don't you? Well you ain't gonna get there without me. (*To the boys.*) You want respect? Live the life you're suppose to? Well you ain't gonna do it without me. There's only one way out of this place and I, Howie Navaroe, knows the way. Who is it who's managed to do what everyone else round here's been trying to do since Risley started running things? Me! Who is it who's got Risley swinging like a kid on a swing? Me! I've done Risley! None a you gonna get anywhere without something bigger and better and I got it!

Brill   You dickhead, Howie Navaroe! Let him phone the ambulance!

Howie   Girls, girls, girls! There at your feet. Is the big man himself. Owner of the Wild at Heart Club, Mr Adam Risley.

Brill   Kenny, you gonna phone or what?

Kenny *makes to go, again* **Howie** *stops him. This time he shoves him out the way.*

Howie   (*to* **Kenny**) Stupid! Stupid! What do you think you're doing? He's our prisoner. You're not suppose to give a toss for prisoners. You're not suppose to call ambulances for them. (*Dragging* **Brill** *from over* **Risley** *and to her feet.*) And you're not suppose to get girls worried over pavement excrement!

Brill   Kenny?

Kenny   Howie mate, come . . .

Howie   Risley's a boss! What do bosses have? Apart from bigger arses for sitting on?

Brill   He needs a doctor!

Howie *ignores* **Brill** *and takes his time.*

Kenny   Howie, for God's sakes, just get to it. Let me go and phone.

Brill   There's a man dying over there.

Hyper   He ain't gonna die, is he Howie?

Howie   He's alright, Hyper.

Kenny   He ain't. Brill's just said . . .

Howie   Shut it! And let me finish what I'm saying. What do bosses have . . . ?

Kenny   He's on about money. Risley's got a safe. Next door. In his office. He's gonna keep him here, beat him senseless until he tells him the combination. He's gonna get the money. Buy some smack, double his money, buy a red Mercedes, propose to Angie and live happily ever after. I can phone now, can I?

Howie *is pissed. He stares* **Kenny** *out. Eventually* **Kenny** *can't look at him and has to look away.*

Brill   I'll go, shall I?

Howie *bars her way as well.*

Brill   Move!

Howie *just stares at her, smiling, as she becomes angrier and angrier.*

Brill   You're a shit, Howie Navaroe, a slimy shit, dragging everyone down in it with you, but not me. I'm gonna count to ten, then I'm gonna scream. One, two, three, four, five, six . . .

Howie *isn't impressed with anything she says and when he begins to grin, all the other lads except* **Kenny** *and* **Sid** *begin to grin.* **Brill** *starts to gather up her things, she's leaving.*

Angie   Is he alright?

Howie *stops grinning and turns to* **Angie**. *They all stop grinning and turn to* **Angie**. *Up until now, she has been silent. Off in her own world.* **Brill** *is still packing.*

Angie   Is he alright?

Howie   What you asking 'bout him for?

Angie   Brill, is he all right?

Brill   I got a life coming to me. I ain't staying round for this.

Angie   He ain't dead, is he?

Brill   I'm going to Edinburgh. I've seen this shit before. I've seen killings and needles and crap, and I ain't friggin' staying round to see it again.

Howie   You're a gobby little bitch, Brill Tyler.

Brill   If being a bitch means not hanging round here sinking in it with you and your shit, then, yes, I'm a bitch.

Angie   Brill, is he dead?

Howie   Course he ain't dead.

Hyper
Lewis } Course he ain't dead.
Fonzo

Howie   (*to* **Angie**) And what you asking about that slag for?

Angie   Is he?

Brill   (*packed, ready to go and meaning it*) I got plans to get out of here, and being sent down for murder's not the way I planned it.

Linda *again tries to say something. She runs over to where* **Risley** *is being held by the lads. She kneels looking at him.* **Angie** *goes over to* **Brill**, *still avoiding looking at* **Risley**. *She grabs* **Brill** *by the arms and stops her.*

Angie   Please, please, just look at him!

Howie   Angela?

Brill   (*shrugging* **Angie** *off her*) No!

Angie *makes another attempt, grabs hold of her again. She is almost crying, but again* **Brill** *pushes her off her.*

Brill   He's dead already. Alright?

Afraid, the lads let go of **Risley** *with little respect and* **Risley** *crashes to the floor. The lads step away, fear all around them.* **Linda** *is over him, searching for signs of life.*

Nadine *and* **Sonia** *grab hold of each other and hold on to each other.*

Howie   You don't kill someone just like that do you? Not with a few slaps. You need guns and knives and stuff. We never used no guns, no knives, no nothing. We tapped him a couple of times. Brill Tyler! All them lies you keep telling, it's got to stop and stop now. You're just trying to scare the shit out of us, aren't you? Angie told me what a bitch you are. I never believed her until now. But now I see for myself, I can't believe she put up with you all these years.

Brill   What you gonna do with the dead body, Howie?

He pushes her to the floor.

Howie   He ain't dead!

Kenny *goes to help her.*

Anyone see Risley move since we came in?

No one can answer him.

Anyone see him move since we brought him in here? Someone must have seen him?

Kenny   Nobody's seen him move, alright? 'We're gonna do this. We're gonna do that.' We're gonna do nothing but go down for this.

Fonzo   Shit! We never said we were gonna kill him.

Hyper   We never said anything like that!

Howie *grabs hold of* **Kenny** *and begins marching him over to* **Risley**.

Howie   You're the clever one, you're the one with your head in them friggin' books every second of the day. You look at him.

Kenny *struggles, but* **Howie** *has hold of him.* **Howie** *throws him down to within inches of* **Risley**'s *face.* **Kenny** *stares at* **Risley**, *petrified at being that close to a dead man.* **Kenny** *slides away on his arse.*

Howie Chicken shit! That's what you are, Kenny Murphy. People like you sponge off people like me. You hang about waiting for people like me to get all the ideas, and then you take the glory. You wanna do stuff, but you're shit-scared. Shit-scared to go to college when you had the chance. Shit-scared to get a life. Shit-scared of your own shadow.

Hyper He ain't really dead, is he, Howie mate?

Howie No he ain't.

Hyper I saw him move. Since we brought him in, I saw him move.

Lewis Did you?

Hyper His fingers moved. Like that.

Hyper *demonstrates with a clenched fist that slowly opens. They all watch.*

Howie (*to* **Brill** *and* **Kenny**) See? See?

Hyper
Fonzo ⎬ We saw his fingers move!
Lewis

Howie And if he can move his fingers, he ain't dead.

Sid Sometimes the body moves after it's dead. It don't mean it's alive.

Lewis 'Sometimes the body moves after it's dead. It don't mean it's alive'? If you move, you're alive, if you don't, you're dead.

Sid I read it someplace, didn't I?

Lewis And that's the trouble with you and him, (*Pointing to* **Kenny**.) you read too friggin' much. You think you could've waved a book under that scumbag's nose (*Pointing at* **Risley**.) when he was doing you tonight?

Sid Just shut up about that, will you?

Lewis Don't want the girls to hear what a fucking hero you been tonight, Sidney?

Sid Just shut up!

Lewis Well I can shut up about it, Sidney, but it don't stop it being true, does it? You got yourself trussed up like a fucking parcel to the Outer Hebrides tonight . . .

Sid Shut up!

Lewis . . . like a fucking parcel to Outer Hebrides! You pissed yourself, almost crapped yourself, and you looked just like my kid sister's puppy Jason. 'Sometimes the body moves after it's dead. It don't mean it ain't dead'?

Howie *moves over to* **Linda**, *stands her up and rips the gag off her mouth. A loud cry bursts from* **Linda**'s *mouth.*

Howie   Alright Miss Bra-Made-A-Brass, what's the combination for the safe? What's the number?

Linda *is sobbing, but* **Howie** *won't let her be. He holds onto her by her clothing imploring her to speak.*

Howie   What's the number? What's the fucking number? Ah? What is it? Ah? Ah? What is it?

Linda   Ask her!

She's looking over at **Angie** *as she speaks. They all look over to where she's looking.* **Angie** *is looking petrified.*

Howie   What?

Linda   Ask her!

Howie *continues to hold on to* **Linda** *by her clothes. He's paralysed as he stares at* **Linda**.

Lewis   (*to* **Howie**) What's she on about?

Angie   Nothing. She's on about nothing!

Howie *still has hold of her.*

Linda   Ask her.

Angie   Shut up!

Linda   Ask her!

Lewis   Ask her what?

Linda   Ask her why she suddenly changed her lying bitching mind, and told you to meet Adam? (*To* **Angie**.) You think a girl would know when a man was just using her, wouldn't you? You think a girl would know when a man was just leading her on, wouldn't you? Wouldn't you? You'd know, wouldn't you, Sonia?

Angie *makes a grab at* **Linda**, *but* **Howie** *stops her.*

Angie   (*to* **Howie**) I need to talk to you.

Howie   (*to* **Linda**) Go on then. Tell us.

Angie   Howie, please let me talk to you.

Howie   (*to* **Linda**) Go on!

Angie   Let me talk to you!

Howie   (*to* **Angie**) What?

Angie   You don't want me to say it here do you? In front of everyone, like?

Howie *shoves* **Linda** *away and she falls to the floor. He turns to* **Angie**.

Linda   She set you up.

Angie *tries to take* **Howie**'s *arm, to lead him away, but he won't be in it. He turns back to* **Linda**.

Linda   That's what last night was all about. Her, changing her mind. She's set you up. She's been doing Risley. You caught them on Castleford Wreck, remember? He wasn't forcing her, he wasn't holding her down, more like the other way round.

Angie   Shut up!

Linda   She's set you up. To get you done and done once and for all! She set you up to get you killed.

Angie   Liar! She's lying, Howie.

Linda   (*to* **Angie**) Adam never wanted you, he never gave a toss about you. You're just a kid, how could he?

Angie   Liar!

Brill   Risley's your new man!

Angie   What new man?

Brill   You bitch!

Angie   Brill, for God's sake!

Nadine   He gave her a ring. She showed it us.

Angie   For Christ's sakes, you two, why're you doing this to me? Why're you saying all this? You've always been jealous of me. (*To* **Howie**) Ask Sonia, she'll tell you, they've always been jealous of me.

Sonia   No they ain't. More like the other way round if you ask me.

Nadine   It's round her neck. It's from Risley.

Brill   He's dead 'cause of you, and all you can do is try and save your skin.

Angie   I didn't do nothing!

Howie *goes to* **Angie** *and tussles with her to get the chain from around her neck. Eventually he succeeds and rips it off. He looks at it. They all stare at her and she stares back at them, full of defiance.*

Angie   (*to all of them*) Satisfied, are you? Satisfied, are you?

Brill   You never meant to go to Edinburgh, did you? It was just all a lie to keep me quiet.

Angie   So! We were never gonna get there. We were never gonna get there no way, no how. Just you and your stupid ideas as usual. Ever since I can remember, you been coming up with them. And they never get us nowhere. And so all we do is hang around waiting for your next stupid idea. Yeah, Edinburgh's stuck round longer than the others, but it's just like the rest of them. It ain't gonna come to nothing. But you don't care, do you? 'Cause it's always me out there, always me with the bulb up my arse, not you. My life ain't funny, Brill. My life is shit! But it ain't gonna be shit forever. I ain't gonna have the kinna life they have round here: babies and drugs, babies and ale. My life's gonna be special. (*To* **Howie**.) And as for you. You're never gonna get that red Mercedes, 'cause you're going nowhere. You might've killed Risley, but God, are you going nowhere. (*To all of them.*) None a you are going nowhere. But I am. 'Cause I got balls and I got guts, I have. Reckon I might even have your balls, Howie mate. You see, you gotta have balls and you gotta have guts to take what you want, when you see it! None a you got balls, none a you got guts. Do any of you really know what you want? Well, I do.

Angie *packs up her stuff and walks out. All of them are left stunned.*

Lewis   What we gonna do Howie mate?

Fonzo $\left.\vphantom{\begin{array}{l}a\\b\end{array}}\right\}$ What we gonna do Howie mate?
Hyper

Howie *just stands there stunned. He doesn't know what they're gonna do.*

Be as Hard as Nails and Give Nothing Away

Jenny McLeod interviewed by Jim Mulligan

At school in Nottingham, Jenny McLeod had an idea that she would like to be a writer, but it seemed such a strange ambition that she kept quiet about it. After all, her mother was a nurse, her father worked on the buses, and her four sisters showed no literary leanings. But when she abandoned her A Level studies to write, her family supported her, and the winning of Writing '87, organised by Nottingham and Derby Playhouses, was the impetus she needed to carry on writing. She has now been writing full-time for eight years and completed ten plays. *The Wild at Heart Club* was commissioned by the Royal National Theatre.

'The play is about two groups of young people who are not exactly members of gangs, but who have decided where their loyalties lie and are committed to each other. I originally saw them as 16 or 17 years old, but people who have read the play see them as older than that. The owner of the club, Risley, is older than the others and preys on them. He fancies himself as being hard and flash; he is what Howie may become if he continues unchecked. Risley thinks money is the answer to everything; that the only way to get on is to be as hard as nails, to give nothing away emotionally or physically.'

One of the questions about *The Wild at Heart Club* that must be resolved at the outset is why a bright, intelligent person like Angie should fall for Risley. Glamour and power are the reason. He has achieved what Angie is determined to achieve: to get out of the little world the young people are trapped in. He has the money, the car, and the designer clothes. He is the hard man that everyone looks up to and, above all, he owns the Wild at Heart Club, which Angie needs if she is to get to Edinburgh. 'Angie knows that her plan to get out by way of the Edinburgh Festival is unrealistic for someone of her age, but she knows she has to get away somehow. Her attachment to Howie started when they were at school, and they've mucked about together for years. She sees that he could be the next Risley, so she is holding on to him for insurance, but she has plans to get rid of him in a very public gesture. Howie is a joke. He only manages to get Risley because his gang find him by chance without his minders.'

The plan which Angie and Risley have hatched is to kill Howie in front of everyone so that Risley can publicly claim Angie. Jenny McLeod's justification for something so extreme is that these things do, in fact, happen. Her play simply explores the consequences of such an act. She sees Angie as taking everything at face value. Angie believes that Risley loves her, that he will claim her, and that they will drive off together in the flash car with the money. She believes that Risley will kill Howie, and she accepts it. 'It's like an adventure to her. They've talked about it. He's told her how he will do it and she's told him how she wants it done, in front of the crowd. On the night, they are still talking about it, and yet there is a little part of her that doesn't believe it will happen. It can only make sense if Angie is still not an adult. Young people of her age do become infatuated by evil people, and occasionally they do the most incredibly violent acts.'

Jenny McLeod is not the sort of person who advocates violence, nor has she experienced anything like what happens in the play. She has known people who take and sell drugs, who have cars and money, but as far as she knows they have never killed. She does not take a moral stand when she writes plays. For her it is enough to tell a story, and if that story involves Flash Harries who have never worked a day in their lives, but who have houses and money, then she will tell the story as vividly as she can without exploring her characters' motives. 'I'm not attracted to these people, I see through them. I know how hard I have to work to make a living writing, and I always wonder about people with money they haven't earned. I have no respect for them. I do not think that, because I portray such people in my plays, I am responsible for anyone who watches the play and aspires to be like them. To say that is to give writers far too much power. If anyone is going to do something wrong as a result of seeing my play, then there was already the propensity for that action before my script came along. I admit I am fascinated by the way some people will kill just as if it was like going to the shops. But all I do is show the effect a violent act has on a character and a situation, and that is as far as it goes.'

The society portrayed is a bleak one. Casual sex, drug usage, exploiting others for drugs, achieving ends by violent means, and people dominating their partners are the norm. But Jenny McLeod says this is a snapshot of how people live. The characters are young, they have just left school or are trying to get some kind of education at college, they do not earn money, they live by their wits.

'At the end, everyone is stunned. Things haven't worked out as they were planned. Howie has lost Angie. Risley might be dead. Brill feels betrayed. They don't know whether to call an ambulance or to run, but there are some positive things. I hope you get the feeling that Angie might use her talents to get out of the situation she is in, that Sonia will find the love she is after, that Sid will get to college, that Brill will become a successful writer. But the hard fact is that, in the society they live in, with the limited opportunities they have, it is very unlikely.'

Jenny McLeod lives in London. Her plays include *Cricket at Camp David* (Nottingham and Derby Playhouses, 1987, and Bolton Octagon, 1988), about life in a difficult West Indian family; *Island Life* (commissioned and toured by Monstrous Regiment in 1988); *Raising Fires* (Bush Theatre, 1994 – winner of the LWT Plays on Stage Award) about the first young black girl in a small community in East Anglia; and *Victor and the Ladies* (to be produced at the Tricycle Theatre in 1995). She has also written *The Wake* for the BBC.

The Wild at Heart Club

Production Notes

Setting and staging

The settings which need to be suggested include a claustrophobic night club and a derelict street. **Music** can be used to build excitement and anticipation, as well as the atmosphere of the club, which might be smokey and hot when crowded. Angie will need a microphone for her 'act'. **Costumes** should reflect the characters' status and individuality (Risley), or lack of individuality (the gangs).

The play needs an urban setting, since the events within it reflect the position of young people attempting to make something of their lives in a frightening and brutal world. What will need examining is the language. The characters in the play swear habitually and casually, and so it will be important to avoid stressing every swear word, which would be unnatural and would upset the rhythm of the language. Another technical consideration will be the **fight sequences**, which will need careful staging.

Elements that will need to be brought out in the story are its pace (everything happens within twenty-four hours), the cult of personality, dreams, drugs, escape, sex, and money. It needs to be raw, gutsy, unreflective, and energised.

Casting

The cast of twelve comprises five women and seven men, aged between sixteen and twenty. Risley appears older and more worldly than the rest.

Questions

1. Why does Angie fall for Risley?

2. Does Angie share Brill's dream of going to Edinburgh?

3. Can Angie be described as a heroine?

4. Which (if any) of the characters is sympathetic? Who is the least sympathetic character?

5. Is Risley dead at the end of the play, or faking it to outwit Howie?

6. Encourage individual actors, in character, to ask themselves:
   i Who am I?
   ii What is the situation?
   iii What do I want from this situation?
   iv What do I want from life?
   v What can I do to achieve (iii) and (iv), given (ii)?
   vi What is my relationship to the other characters?
   vii Which of my lines illustrate (vi)?

    viii   Apart from speaking the line appropriately, how else can I express on stage the answers to the above questions?

Exercises

1.   A lot of tension exists between the characters in the play and through the changing circumstances in which they find themselves. There are dozens of ways to say a line. Take 'I love you'. Experiment with different approaches – e.g. 'I love *you*'. or '*I* love you'. It can be said in an insincere way, to get its opposite meaning. Introduce a pause after 'love' and suspense is added. Find ways to *create* and not *impose* tension.

2.   In character, create a 'freeze-frame' which depicts the relationships and the tension that exists between the characters. Briefly talk through the immediate and longer-term personal histories. Create scenes that explain how current tensions came about.

3.   *Status*
      i   Status varies in the gangs. Take each character and give her or him a number from ten to zero, ten representing the highest possible status. Chart each character's journey through the play. Are there any points at which their status drops or is raised? Decide why this happens.
      ii In pairs, A = male (status 8), B = female (status 2). Take only three minutes to improvise a situation where the pair exchange status, so that the female's status is raised to 8, and the male's reduced to 2. Repeat the exercise using different combinations, e.g. female starts at 8 and male at 2, both are female and equal status, and use different situations. Identify points in the play where the characters' status is challenged.
      iii Take the character Risley and seat him on a chair. Have the other characters approach him and experiment with ways in which they would react if Risley stands, speaks, or moves towards them. Repeat the exercise, substituting other characters for Risley, and concentrating on both dialogue and body language.
      iv Have the female characters in the play form a group and describe how their ideal man/least ideal man would look and behave. Have the male characters do the same exercise describing their ideal/least ideal woman.

4.   *Combat Excercises*
Take time to work out the violent scenes carefully. Look at fight sequences in films on video, freezing the action and slowing it down. Make sure you are working in a safe environment when choreographing your own. Ask the participants always to make eye contact before making a move, and be certain to work from a safe distance. Concentrate on creating a convincing effect through skill and commitment.

Suzy Graham-Adriani
Director/Producer for BT National Connections

The Minotaur

Jan Maloney

Author's note

The Chorus text may be divided among the individuals in the Chorus as suits each production. Additionally, the Chorus can physically represent settings such as the ship and the labyrinth.

The Minotaur was commissioned and first performed by Contact Youth Theatre, Manchester, while Jan Maloney was writer-in-residence there.

Act One

Scene One

Chorus *of fourteen, seven men and seven women on the harbour beside a ship with black sails.*

Chorus
Our fate is sealed.
Our fate is sealed.
We're off to Crete
To die at the feet
Of their monstrous god.
Get a good look around you.
You'll never see Athens' shore again.
The busy streets, the lapping waves,
The grey-green olive trees above the town,
The Acropolis proud.
Old Aegeus smug in his powerlessness.
It's not his son that has to go.
Oh no! We are left weaponless.
We are left helpless.
My mother's weeping now.
My father's wailing now.
I can't look him in the eye.
Aegeus counts his son too high.
So long he's longed for one.
He was putty in Medea's hands
For want of a son.
None of them'll go, of that you may be sure.
None of the sons of Pallas,
Or Medea's brats. Oh no.
And especially not Theseus.
Can't spill royal blood,
That wouldn't do, would it?

They move onto the ship.

We're penned like cattle
And prodded to make us go.
And all to feed he who is half-cattle himself.
I wanted to be a smith,
I was learning the craft.
Metalwork. I was an apprentice,
Just begun. . . .

Crete's the place for metalwork, my son.
Don't call me that.
They wrought great inventions from bronze
An alloy of copper and tin. I know that.
Well now you may see them.
See them? What good is that to me?
I'll be a pile of bones
Left on the labyrinth floor.
Some say we may have a chance.
A chance of slavery
Or a chance of death,
To wait for us in the shape
Of a beastly fiery bull
Waiting on its hunger.
It can't feed on fourteen of us at once.
I was to marry in the spring.
What would be worse?
For her to grow old and wear widow's weeds
Or for her to find a new young man
Not cursed by Cretan greed
Or Athenian folly.

Enter **Aegeus**.

Aegeus
The lot is cast, yet the deed is not yet done.
You have the journey yet to come and to endure.
Don't think I don't know how you all must feel
Beneath black sails, going to certain death.
The boat is stocked with delicacies and wine,
Diverse games and distractions grace the hold.
You are laying down your life, not for your king,
But so Athenians may live, may breathe, may sing!
So hold your head proud and be noble in your heart.
Untie the ropes, it's time for you to part.

Theseus *bursts in.*

Theseus
Hold it. Wait for me. I'm going.

Aegeus
No, son, the lot is cast.

Chorus
You bet your life it is.

Theseus
Father, I cannot let Athenians go and die
On foreign soil while I await your pleasure

Here at home. You kept this from me.
Distracted me with gifts and errands,
So I may not know what's going on.
As I am your son, I must know everything important
And yet you treat me like a child.

Aegeus
You are indeed still very young.

Theseus
And them? Do they look like my elders?

Points to **Chorus**.

Hardly. Hardly a full-grown beard amongst them
And each girl a virgin. If that's true, they
Can't be so very old that I can't share their fate.
The rock I heaved and levered out the ground
So that my fingers burst and bled.
The sword I found and by which
I claimed you as my father –
Was that sword passed on to me
For cowering here in Athens
While Athenians die on foreign soil?
No. It was not.

Aegeus
The lot is cast, the numbers up.
Fate's played its part and justice done.
It can't be changed now, it cannot be undone.

Theseus
What's done can be undone.
That's a fact everybody knows.
Until these men lie mauled and lifeless
At the Minotaur's gnarled and hairy feet,
Change is a wind can blow
And fate a box of tricks to be upturned.
Which of you men is man enough
To let me go face the beast in your place,
To see who has the bravery to stand down,
The grace to not be brave.

Male Solo Chorus
I don't see why it shouldn't be me
Seeing as you put it like that.

Thesues
Good. The weakest link in the chain
Has snapped. Now you may go

And may the gods be good to you.
You'll need it, but not as much as us,
For we have work to do that needs no
Cowards. We've fighting, thinking, feeling,
All to do together.
Now hoist the sail and let's away.

Aegeus
So you mean to fight great Crete.
You are headstrong and I love you for it.
But when you see the palace walls,
Hear the bull-man-beast roar,
When you inhale the exotic incense of Cretan shores,
When you feel the dark power of their seas,
When you taste the blood . . .

Theseus
Have you been there?

Aegeus
No, but I've heard tell.

Theseus
Well, I'm going there and I'll be coming back.

Aegeus
I doubt it, son, but if you do,
Don't sail back with those
Dreaded Cretan black sails.
They've always brought on the shiver that is death.
Put up white sails so we may know
You have survived by some tangle of fate.
For you'll not manage it alone.
White sails! Bring them to me!
Quickly, before they go. Bring me white sails.

The freed boy of the **Chorus** *runs and gets them and throws them on the black-sailed ship just in time.*

Scene Two

Male Chorus
We are just pawns in a political game.
Disposable peasants, that's all we are to them.
So they feed us up and send us off
With wine and feastings,
Games to wile away the time.

They pat our backs and tell us heroic tales
And, giving sheepish looks,
Pack us off to certain death.

Chorus
Don't mind us, we're just the Chorus,
Drafted to far-off Crete
To keep old Minos sweet
Just cos his wife got screwed by a bull.
Can you imagine?
Talk about horny!
Got that Daedalus to build that maze
To hide her shame.
Should have killed her there and then
If you ask me.
Mind you, if I got screwed by a bull
That'd do me in.
Can you imagine?

Theseus
Come on, let's drink.
The sun's beginning to go down.
Let's light the lamps. Fetch the unwatered wine.

Chorus
Let's get it while we can,
For our death looms
As certain as the sun
Will rise tomorrow out the sea.
I smell the aroma of curdled fruit,
Dear to Dionysus.

Theseus
You're right.
Death is certain.

Pause.

But it's not as certain when or how she'll strike.
That is not for us to know.
I've thought myself set for certain death before now
And the great god has proven me wrong.

Chorus
Zeus can never be trusted.

Theseus
No, I am Poseidon's son.

Chorus
Poseidon. Poseidon. Poseidon.
You follow him.

Theseus
I follow him, yes, sometimes,
And sometimes he follows me.

Chorus
By the gods, you're cocksure.
You'll bring the waves against us
Crashing. You'll make him brew up
A storm. Talking like that.
Have respect.

Theseus
I respect him as a son does his father.

Chorus
Death by drowning . . .
Every time I look up
The black sail flapping.
Crow's wing. Funeral cloth,
Shivers over the water
Lapping into my bones.
The shiver of death,
Death by drowning.
If this dark ship of fodder for the beast
Got caught in some freak typhoon
And whirlwinded down some black hole of the sea
Then the Minos bull would eat no Athenians.
I'd rather death by drowning than face the dance of death.

Theseus
Have faith in Poseidon.
The waves are fair tonight
And don't forget he rules the earth too.

Chorus
In Crete, too, yes. He's the bull-god, he's theirs . . .

Theseus
He's ours too.
We must make him ours, all of us.
It is our only chance. He makes the earth shake.

Chorus
Yes, like the Minotaur.
And more. He makes earthquakes.
He makes volcanoes erupt.
He changes the shape of the world.

Theseus
Exactly. And that's what we need
And in that we must trust.

They are now beginning to get a bit drunk.

Theseus
That's what we're doing.
That's what I was doing when I found the sword.
Knew it was mine and that Aegeus,
King of Athens, waited for me.
I went to him.
I didn't go by sea.
He had so many men,
The sons of Pallas,
Warring for the throne.
Nephews, great-nephews.

Chorus
At least they're legitimate.
It's more than you are.

Theseus
I am according to Poseidon.
And a god's law
Is above and beyond
Mere man's law.

Chorus
Don't mind us,
We're mere mortals.

Theseus
He'd nearly given up on me ever arriving.

Chorus
What kept you?

Theseus
Had to clear the Isthmus Road of brigands,
Had to put down villains who would make
Your flesh creep just to hear of them.

Chorus
No thanks, I've got enough on my plate
With the present predicament,
If it's all the same to you.

Theseus
Suit yourself.
But I still have that sword.

Chorus
That's typical. We all had ours
Snatched away.

Theseus
I came so late
And unpremeditated.
I got away with it.
But I hereby swear,
As Poseidon rules the sea
My sword shall be put to
The service of you all.
I shall not save myself with it
Unless I save each
And every one of you.

Chorus
It has the snakes on it.
It is the royal sword.
He did come of his own accord,
Much against his father's wishes.

Female Solo
The sea, so still, so serene,
The sunset glorious,
Beauty, calm, teasing us.
The way he looks at me.
The meeting of eyes guarding disturbed souls
Hiding insufficiently the fear.
Oh yes, I've caught Theseus
With the hollow look in his eyes
Which lies
Of what's within.

The women start to play music and dance.

He, of all of us, cannot show
That within which we already know.
The roar, the dark, the pounce, the pain,
Oblivion threatens again and again.
No, my soul doesn't yearn for the heroic Theseus,
But rather the scared Theseus, the insecure Theseus,
Who stares out soulfully to sea
And hopes we do not see
His quaking fear.
If I did live, if I had the choice,
He would be the one for me.

Chorus
You cannot take one of the bull-girls here.
If they arrive on Cretan shores
Found to not be virgins,
They are publicly humiliated and killed.
No waiting for the Minotaur's hunger
Or a chance
At the bull dance
Or whatever goes on.
We will not know till we arrive.
To spend your last days
Under the sun and moon and stars
With seven young Athenian virgins
Who, through honour, you dare not screw.
What torture is this?
Worse than being mangled by the monster,
Of that I'm sure.
Of course, at night, after drinking wine
It's easy to let honour fly away
With resolutions made by sober day.
But if we are caught
We'd be thrown overboard to drown
And they'd go back for replacements.
A dishonour too great.
Imagine how your mother and father would feel.

Theseus
Yes. I'm dying for it too, and, so, you know,
Are they. But we must take our lust and weave it
Into a yarn of strength,
To bind us as a team.
We will not go then with heads bowed
And eyes wondering,
Mouths falling open at their splendid ways.
We cannot fuck, but we can dance with them.

They all dance together until they collapse. One man and one woman from the **Chorus**
stand up, kiss, hold hands and walk away intertwined and in secret.

Scene Three

Theseus *on board ship looking out to sea.*

Theseus
O, Poseidon,
Island maker,

Earth shaker,
Volcano blaster
Ocean master!
When storms rage
And the tide pulls,
When horses race
And men fight bulls,
Poseidon, you are there.
Power Poseidon
Poseidon power
Help me, empower me,
Strengthen me now.
Lend me your power
Poseidon power
Poseidon as father
Poseidon as god,
I offer you allegiance
Give me your strength to face the beast's gaze.
Give me your power to unravel the maze.
Filling the convoluted ways
With river power
Flowing wherever it goes.
Give me the bravery to face my foes.

Minos *appears out of the sea wearing a bull mask.* **Chorus** *thinks he is Poseidon and pray with their palms flat on the deck.*

Theseus
Oh, my God!

Minos
Half-god, half-human and the human half's royal.
And you're the little upstart claiming Poseidon
Of all the gods to be your father!
Calling him up as if he were yours to call in such a way.
Poseidon has always been hand-in-glove with Crete.

Chorus *realize he's not Poseidon and stop praying.*

Theseus
And much more if tales are to be believed
Of your wayward queen and a certain bull.
An embodiment of Poseidon, was it not?

Minos
Insult me not, Athenian runt.
Did you not see how Poseidon guides me through the deep?
Will he do as much for you?

Theseus
Surely, he is my father, so he would.

Minos
I hope your logic's good.
Now, see this ring . . .

He takes a ring from his finger and holds it up on high.

If you be fathered by Poseidon, he will be your guide.
Dive for it and return it to me here.
Do not return without it, rather drown than grace the deck
Of this black-sailed boat without that ring.
You understand?

Theseus
Indeed I do. Your challenge does not disturb me.
Throw down the ring into the deep.
I'll follow it and like some dolphin command the sea
And reach down to the sea bed and find the trinket
And bring it back to you, King Minos.

Minos *throws the ring and* **Theseus** *takes off a top layer of clothes and sword and dives after it.*

Chorus
The sea's so deep here,
Far away from any land.
He's Aegeus' son, isn't he?

Solo
That's what he said in Athens.
Whichever suits, it seems to me.

Solo
I can't believe he'll find it.
In amongst the weeds, slithering fish and coral reef.

Female Solo
There's no sign of him yet.

Minos *picks up* **Theseus**'s *sword while the* **Chorus** *looks out to sea and hides it under his cloak.*

Solo
Poseidon may be powerful but why should he help him?
Surely he's got better things to do.

Female Solo
There's still no sign of him.

Chorus
He'll be gasping,
Grasping out for air,
Kicking, struggling,
With weight of water
All around.

Female Solo
There's no sign of him at all.

Minos
That's the thing with someone like Theseus.
He can't resist a challenge.
Demand he does the impossible
And full of gallantry and downright arrogance,
He'll have a go.

Female Solo
There, that must be him.

Solo
It is.
Red and gasping out for breath.
It is him.
He's swimming this way.

Minos
He'll have returned without it,
Mark my words,
But with some fancy story
To wrap his failure in.

Theseus *struggles onto the deck and collapses, gasping, trying to get his breath back.*
They wait. **Theseus** *stands up, faces* **Minos** *and hangs his head slightly.*

Minos
Come on, let's have it then.

Theseus *holds up his finger bearing the ring.* **Theseus** *reveals the ring and gives it to*
Minos. **Minos** *inspects it.*

Theseus
Now do you believe me?
I'm guided by gods
And they guide me to Crete,
To Knossos, to the labyrinth,
And they'll guide me through
To the centre where there cowers
The royal shame,
That dark and dreadful curse,

The crossbreed that should have died at birth.
He may bellow all he likes.
You may threaten all you like.
I'm coming and I'm out to get you,
Minos, King of Crete
And ruler, till now, of all the seas around.
Your power is waning,
The sand is running out.
You've overstepped the mark,
Harbouring some monster born
Out of nature,
Born by deception.

Minos
Insult my land no more, boy.
When you arrive, you will be fed to my Minotaur
Like everyone else on board this ship.
Till then, I advise each and every one of you
To get drunk. It may take the edge off the indescribable pain
And dull the panic induced by waiting.

Pause.

And, Theseus, give me the ring.

Theseus
Keep the sword, but . . .

Minos (*sarcastic*)
Oh, thank you.

Theseus
The ring, you dedicated to Poseidon
By throwing it down to the ocean deep.
He bids me guard it for him.
I'll return it when we arrive on Cretan shores.

Minos
That'll not be long,
And anyway, I own you.

Theseus
Oh, yes, I forgot.

Minos
Not for long

Minos *takes the sword and disappears into the sea.*

Chorus
Now we've not one sword amongst us.
Tricked out of weapon and birthright

In one flail swoop.
So much for dedicating it
To fight for one and all!

Theseus *stares out to sea.*

Chorus
Maybe we should have a little faith.
He did retrieve the ring and wears it still.
I couldn't sleep last night,
Even though I was drunk.
I couldn't sleep last night.
When I shut my eyes I saw
The dark corridors meandering,
Heard the bull-man-beast roar,
Felt the presence of his power.
I had to light the light.
I couldn't sleep last night.

Chorus
Sea all around and not a hint of land.
If I close my eyes I fear the dark.
If I open them I just feel sick.

Scene Four

Crete comes into view.

Chorus
The harbour's deep and full of ships.
Each sail so dark it could be a funeral barge.
Just like the one we all sail in now.
The palace so grand
And sporting bulls' horns,
Line upon line of them
Against the sparkling sky.
But beneath that splendour
The convoluted labyrinth
Snakes its evil way
Designed by Daedalus.
Don't say that name to me.
Turncoat working for the other side
And so may you be soon, to save your skin.
But I'm not some genius inventor, like him.
I'm not a man who can make magic
Such as this out of some rogue metal.
I can't play with shapes, numbers and concepts

Like they be so much wool for a kitten to toy with.
Deep in the bowels of that fair place
Murder in the dark lurks,
By some freak of nature
Bellowing in the bowels of that fair place.
Hidden, horrid, craving human flesh
Which the beast demands from all the world.
Crete wants our brains, our souls,
Our hearts to feed to its beast.
Why do they want to squeeze out our humanity
On a lost cause?
How could they be so power-mad?
And need to prove their power
By an act of such futility?

The town comes fully into view.

Glorious city. It makes Athens
Look like toy town.
Look, the grandeur and the size.
I thought what I'd heard was a load of lies.
But, no, the splendour, look, it's clear from here.

Theseus
Now is the time to sing
The song to show our pride.
Now is not the time
To gawp or shake or hide.
Stand up and in the sober light
Of afternoon perform the song which
We invented last night.
Now, clear the decks,
And keep your heads up, peacock-high.

Chorus
The music. Come on.
Breathe deep.
Show no fear.
Indeed, feel none.
Sing like you mean it.
And have fun.

Music, singing.

Act Two

Scene One

Minos *on a plinth with a bull mask.* **Ariadne** *behind a veil, posing as the snake goddess. The dance finishes and they put down their instruments and then step on to the Cretan shore and get their land legs. The Cretan guard moves amongst them and then returns to* **Minos**. **Minos** *sends him back, pointing out* **Theseus**. *The guard tries to get the ring from* **Theseus**. **Theseus** *addresses* **Minos**.

Theseus
King Minos, we meet again
And I said I would return the ring
And so I will to him that you
Dedicated it to when we met out
In the turmoil that is the sea.

Theseus *runs towards the sea and hurls the ring overarm so it goes down into the harbour.*

Minos
Stop that boy!

Theseus
Should you want it, being Poseidon's own
You only need to dive.

Minos
Into a filthy rotting harbour, no.
The sea in port will stink
With stuff turned overboard.

Theseus
You mean beneath this calm surface
All is rotting debris – what a surprise!

Minos
Get that ring!

Theseus
I'll 'get that ring,' as you so delicately say,
When you've returned my sword.
Won hard as my birthright,
It says I'm king.

Chorus
Please calm down.

You put our lives on the line
When you throw yourself recklessly against his will.

Minos
Take the dancing girls away and lock them up.
I've done with bandying words
With that squirt who would be king
Of his thirteen as he can't lead a nation.

Scene Two

Ariadne *enters her sanctuary. She puts down four bowls of milk for the snakes at the edge of the snake pit. They come up and lap the milk. She picks up two snakes, one in each hand and moves round and round the pit, the snakes at her feet.*

Ariadne
Goddess of the ever-changing moon
Goddess of dreams spoken when awake
Goddess of the virgin kept for god
Goddess of the secret-knowing snake.
All is not right. A man has entered here doing evil deeds.
I am all virgin, saved for you
Who bellows beyond the darkness
Of the deep.
I am all virgin saved for you
Beast, brother, god, lover,
Can you hear me nightly weep?

The six young Athenian girls and **Theseus**, *dressed as a girl and wearing a lion skin, walk in, facing her like a shuffling identity parade and she faces them, concentrating, a snake writhing in each hand.*

Ariadne
All go, except you with bare feet.

They exit

Ariadne
Virginity isn't a word which springs to mind.

Theseus *walks towards her and a snake bites his ankle. He yells, revealing that he's male by his voice.*

Ariadne
No man's allowed in here,
The inner sanctuary of the goddess.
This is where I hear the oracles.
I had a feeling a man had been here.

Theseus
I thought there was an exception for royalty.

Ariadne
Oh, it's you, heir to the Athenian throne
And thorn in my father's side.

Theseus
Your feeling was right, oh wise young goddess,
A man had been here.
It was intuition, not premonition.

Ariadne
Or maybe both. But soon you'll die.

Theseus
Or maybe you could save me. Though it's undeserved.
Your father came in here and hid my sword.

Ariadne
How do you know Minos entered here?

Theseus
Poseidon revealed the scene to me
As I threw his ring into the sea.
Is there an antidote to this?

Ariadne
Only one, which I will deliver if your story's proved.
Where is this sword, then?

Theseus
It may have been moved
But as I saw it he hid it in
The deep snake pit.

Ariadne *leaps up and jumps onto a rope.*

Theseus
Ariadne, wait.

She climbs down into the snake pit.

Theseus
It is wrought most wonderfully
With snakes encircling the hilt.
How come you don't get stung?
Because they know you are their
Goddess, I suppose.

Ariadne
No, a simple series of vaccinations as a child.

Theseus
The sting is biting deep.
The poison, I can feel it creep.
Can you see it?
I fear my time is to be cut short
By a grovelling snake
When I have already overcome
Great warriores, a mad giant sow . . .

Ariadne
I found it

*She climbs up with the sword and kneels at his feet and bites out the snake bite. He yells.
She licks around the wound, spits it out and licks his ankle again. He pulls her up and
kisses her on the lips. They embrace passionately, surrounded by snakes.*

Ariadne
I pronounce you not a virgin.

Theseus
No, but I'd be faithful from now on
To you, should you only give me the chance.
I can't believe it, in truth, that such a charmed fate should be mine.
To be taken into the arms of a goddess.
Indeed I hope too high.
I must be fevered from the bite
Of your faithful friend,
Protecting her mistress from the
Approaches of a mere Athenian
And a man to boot, in this
Most holy of sanctuaries.

Ariadne
Theseus, hush, or my mother will hear.

Ariadne *points to the snake pit.*

Ariadne
Down there.

Theseus
Oh, I see.

Ariadne
I will keep this sword,
Place it back where it was . . .

Theseus
But, sweet, it is my symbol of royalty.
By it I claim the thone of Athens,
And my lovely . . .

Ariadne
Yes, and I shall claim my queenship
By a ring you flung into the harbour.

Theseus
Sweet, I'll return it to you.
I took it from your father,
Not from you.
I wouldn't harm a hair on your head
Nor a snake, even though one bit me.
No, I thank it for biting me
For it means I'll have the memory
Of kissing you.
I'll take that to my death.

Ariadne
No, not your death.
Don't mention it.
It strangely stirs my heart
And makes me short of breath.
I'll come to you tonight.
I can't have your death.
I will help you, show you how.
I'll bring the sword, goodbye (*Pause*) for now.

She takes the sword and goes down the rope to the snake pit. **Theseus** *re-adjusts his girl's clothing and joins the* **Chorus**.

Scene Three

Chorus *in dungeons getting ready to try and sleep. Some play 'Knife, Papyrus, Stone'. Others plaiting one another's hair. Enter* **Theseus**.

Chorus
We thought we'd never see you again.
How did you get away with it? Do tell.

Theseus
I like wearing this.
It seems to bring me luck.

Chorus
Your luck is mine.
You saved my skin.

Theseus
Only needed to because
You couldn't save your own.

Solo Female Chorus *takes off his clothes and he takes off hers.* **Theseus** *left in minimum clothing and lion skin wrapped about him.*

Chorus
Did you get guidance from the gods?

Pause.

What's this luck, then, princely one?

Theseus
Too soon to say.

Chorus
Let's try to sleep.
For tomorrow we will need our wits about us.
It may be our last day with wits,
Or even life pulsing through our veins.
Have you heard the bull-man roar?
You should have seen those snakes.
Can she hear the oracle, I wonder?
It was like Delphi, wasn't it?
I bet she can see round corners
Through time and space.
She was weird, wasn't she?
Hid within her snaking charm
Was something I can't quite explain.
Did you charm her, Theseus?
Or did she charm you with her snakes?

Theseus *wrapped in the lion skin as if asleep.*

Chorus
We must try to rest.
Though when I shut my eyes
The blobs are red as blood.
My heart yearns for the Athenian shore
Beyond the yawning of the sea.
The rhythmic bobbing of the white-sailed
Boats, huddled in Athens' homely port.
Athene, fair and wise,
With owl-eyes looking over our city.
We do at least discuss what's going on
Fairness is the goal for which we strive.
We are not weighed down with rituals weird and dark.
Weird and dark. Weird and dark. Weird and dark.
Even at night when drunkenness
May stagger through our streets,
Still the night owl looks on

And sees fair play.
The slaves have freedoms
Unknown anywhere in all the world
Bar Athens.
My mother will be staring out to sea.
My father will be supping watered wine.
My sister will be dreaming of the dark.
My brother will be playing on his pipes
A mournful tune to keep the house awake.
We were forced against our will.
Theseus chose to come,
To meet the beast, to face it, head on.
Now sleep and face the dark
Relax, let go of fear
And even, also, maybe hope.
Flow with it and let the Fates
Take us along
But let us be willing to believe
There is a chink of light
In every deep black night.

They fall asleep.

Scene Four

The **Chorus** *are sleeping.*

Ariadne
Theseus. It's me.

Theseus *looks up.* **Ariadne** *beckons. They tiptoe off.*

Theseus
What do you want?

Ariadne
Want? I want to help you. I meant what I said. I can help you escape.

Theseus
I can't do that. I can't creep away in the night and leave my friends to be savaged by your monster.

Ariadne
I know that. I've brought your sword.

Theseus
I thought you carried it in self-defence.

Ariadne
What? Against you?

Theseus
I am the enemy.

Ariadne
I forgot.

Theseus
We can never forget that.

Ariadne
If I help you, if I give you this sword and tell you how to find your way out of the labyrinths, should you survive . . .

Theseus
I will survive.

Ariadne
If I help you, will you take me away from here?

Theseus
You don't like it here?

Ariadne
It's shadowed over. Old sins. Old mistakes. Secrets hidden away. Old gods half buried but still alive and scratching. No, I want the fresh air of Athens. Thought, new inventions, the meetings of minds . . .

Theseus
And hearts?

Ariadne
We'll have to see, won't we? I know I'd like to go to Athens at your side. I am a princess. I've been trained to rule.

Theseus
But not to serve?

Ariadne
If I were your queen . . .

Theseus
Would you?

Ariadne
Yes, I think I would.

Theseus *pulls her to him. They kiss. The sword gets in the way.*

Theseus
You're not used to carrying a sword, are you?

Theseus *takes the sword off her.*

Ariadne
Now, do you promise?

Theseus
I'll take you away from here, sweet Ariadne. And make you queen – well, only when I become king, of course.

Ariadne
Of course.

Theseus
It could bring peace to all as well as joy to us.

Ariadne
That's what I hope.

Theseus
So, my sweet, how do I escape this labyrinth, once the deed is done? What secret code or mathematical equation, what new-fangled homing device or information storage system?

Ariadne *produces a ball of red string from her pocket.*

Theseus
What?

Ariadne
Wherever you go, whatever route you take, unwind it, leave it on the ground. It'll lead you all the way . . .

Theseus
Home.

Ariadne
Well, back to me. I'll stand and wait for you. I'll hold the end.

Theseus
And then?

Ariadne
We'll collect the others and be off by black of night.

Theseus
Now you promise. No alarms, no tricks, no crying out to Daddy. No changes of mind . . . ?

Ariadne
Or heart. I promise. And you, you promise, you will take me with you?

Theseus
I promise.

They embrace.

Theseus
Now, my sweet princess, let's get going, we haven't got all night.

Ariadne
But there will be many nights . . .

Theseus
Oh, yes.

Theseus *gently takes the red string from her hand. They walk to entrance of the maze.*

Scene Five

Theseus *and* **Ariadne** *stand at the entrance of the labyrinth.*

Ariadne
Tread carefully. My mother is down here.

Theseus
I thought you said she was in the snake pit.

Ariadne
They are one and the same.

Theseus
Oh!

Ariadne
You are going to take me away?
I can't stay here and face the fate
I'd face after the Minotaur was dead.

Theseus
Ariadne, I love you,
I want you to rule Athens with me
And maybe all of Attica and Crete as well
The extent of our empire, it's too soon to tell.
My ambition is great but I see the future
With you by my side. And consider it much the greater for that.

Ariadne
Face him with his fate.
And if you face him
He will deep down believe
And though he fights,
He'll know his time's arrived

Deep in his dark and restless soul.
Now go, and feel me here,
We're linked by means of this red yarn
And however convoluted is the way
I'll be waiting at the end of it for you.

They kiss. He goes, armed with sword. As he goes, he faces axes/lights/mirrors and is often scared by the face he sees in the mirrors. Snakes appear and make **Theseus** *even more jumpy. He is scared of being bitten and their writhing movement gives him a feeling of disorientation. He gradually realises they are following the line of the red string back, away from him and towards* **Ariadne***.*

Pasiphae *is huddled up asleep in the maze and as* **Theseus** *passes she wakes up but doesn't see him. She sees the red string and follows it back with the snakes until she meets* **Ariadne** *standing at the entrance to the maze holding the end of the red string and surrounded by snakes.*

Pasiphae
What's this?

Pasiphae *jolts the string from her hand.*

What's this, eh? Some trick?

Ariadne
No, well, yes. I'm trying it out.
It should work, shouldn't it?
Daedalus told me that's how to find your way out.
A long time ago.
I'm trying it out.

Pasiphae
I know my way round it like I'm a blind woman.
Try living in it like we do.
This is all he's ever known.
Can you even imagine that?
I think not, frankly, I think not.

Ariadne
I can actually. I've been his only visitor.
Remember that. Who else ever came to see him,
To see him grow?

Pasiphae
A womb within a womb.
This place, dark and damp.
You weren't here when he first kicked.
You never touched me.

Ariadne
Not that you would have let me.

Pasiphae
You never visited till he was born.
You couldn't resist that, could you?
Your peep-show mentality.
You always had a cruel streak.

Ariadne
How could you say that?

Pasiphae
Listen, girl, do you think I'm stupid?
I may be locked away from the light,
Abandoned by the man who had more brain cells
Than the lot of them put together.
But I kept up with him, I can assure you.

Ariadne
Daedalus! He caused all the trouble.
He should never have given in to your demands.

Pasiphae
You do. Why shouldn't he?
Anyway I blame your father.

Ariadne
That makes no sense at all.

Pasiphae
I didn't fall in love with a bull.
What do you think I am?
Some beastly nymphomaniac or something? No.
No, I am not. I am a queen.
And I'm still a queen.
I fell in love with a god!
Poseidon dwelt within my bull –
Pure white he was and eyelashes!
I always remember his eyelashes.
He sort of batted them at me.
The darling!

Ariadne
You were in some fake cow Daedalus had knocked up.
How come you saw his eyelashes?

During the following speech we see the Minotaur or his shadow elsewhere in the maze. He is huge and crouched over a low stone slab which is flat but womb-shaped as seen from above. On it are human intestines and offal. The Minotaur's hand dwarfs them as he eats them as a small snack.

Theseus *gradually aproaches the Minotaur as he holds his sword gradually more aloft and overcomes his fears of his reflections and the snakes.*

Pasiphae
We'd courted. We'd been meeting.
It didn't just happen overnight.
I fell in love with him.
Poseidon told your father the bull would come
Out of the frothing waves.
And he did. Poseidon, straight out of the sea. Pure.
Your father should have sacrificed the bull –
My bull. That had been agreed with Poseidon.
But, your father, thinking himself, quite falsely,
Above the rule of gods,
Tried to outwit the great and glorious power of all the sea.

The Minotaur has eaten the guts. He becomes aware of a strange presence, stands up and starts to trample the ground. The tremors are felt by everyone in the labyrinth.

Can you imagine?
He always was a fool.
He went and sacrificed some other bull instead.
Spilt the bull's blood on the altar,
And left the god-bull amongst us, living, breathing,
Full of unharnessed power, all the power of tides
Seethed as that bull's breath seeped in and out,
Rocking, roaring, bellowing with all the force of earth spin.
His eyes glowed like every shimmer of beauty you have ever seen.
Sunsets, mother-of-pearl, kingfishers,
Love in the eye of the one you love.

Ariadne
Mother, I . . .

Theseus *arrives in the centre of the maze and sees the Minotaur.* **Theseus** *steps on the stone slab to reach the Minotaur and his feet get covered in blood. The Minotaur backs up warily at the sight of the sword and disappears into the shadows.* **Theseus** *follows, shaky but brave.*

Pasiphae
He's your brother, girl.

They hear the sound of fighting.

Pasiphae
Who have you let in here?

Pasiphae *runs towards the centre of the maze by the most direct route, not paying attention to the red string.* **Ariadne** *follows her. The hidden fight becomes louder.*
Pasiphae *and* **Ariadne** *arrive so they can see the fight but the audience can't.*

Pasiphae
I carried him.
My god, he was a weight.
I thought he'd kill me,
He was such a weight.
Now may he kill you.
How could you do it to me, Ariadne?
Let the enemy into here of all places? And armed with a sword.

Ariadne
Mother, I . . .

Pasiphae
Shut up! I gave birth to him somehow.
God, the pain.
Daedalus stayed for that.
Stitched me up
With a needle and some stuff he used to makes those wings
Which sped him off and away from me.
Stop him. Get the sword off him for godsake.

Ariadne
Mother, I'm in love with him.

Pasiphae
Is that your excuse?

Ariadne
Well, it was yours.

Pasiphae
Love for a god – not my enemy.

Ariadne
One day he will be king.

Pasiphae
Of Athens.

Ariadne
Daedalus was Athenian.

Pasiphae *grabs her and throws her towards the fight.*

Pasiphae
Get that sword off him.
Athenian, drop your sword
And I will save your life.
Spare my son.
I suckled him.

I weaned him.
Stopped him eating away
At my very breasts.
It was I who realized what he needed.
Human flesh.
I love him so much.
I've seen him grow up.
Walking on all fours and then on two.
Spare him.

Ariadne *is pushed out in view of the audience, splattered with blood.*

Pasiphae
Get the sword, you bitch.

Pasiphae *goes to strangle* **Ariadne**.

Pasiphae
Spare my son or I will kill her here and now.
Have you ever fucked him? Have you?

Ariadne
No, he's my brother.
I wouldn't dream of it.

Ariadne *gets out of her grip and they fight.*

Pasiphae
So like your father, quick to lie.
Each one a poison arrow.
He's a very good lover.
The half-beast being half-god,
To be highly recommended.

Ariadne
Mother, you disgust me.

Pasiphae
And your disgust disgusts me.
He's dying, my son, my god, my lover
All that is left to me.
And you, you treacherous, conniving,
Underhand bitch,
You give me moral lectures.
How could you?

The Minotaur bellows a bass note of pain which is reflected by **Pasiphae**'s *treble screams of agony.* **Theseus** *kills the Minotaur.* **Pasiphae** *continues to scream.*
Theseus *approaches the stone slab holding the Minotaur's guts which are three times the*

size of the human ones which were there before. He throws them over the stone slab, and they completely cover it.

Theseus
Poseidon, Father,
The Minotaur I dedicate to you.
As his heart stops beating
Know it is for you.

Theseus *looks carefully at the arrangement of the Minotaur's guts and uses them as an augury.*

Theseus
Take the head . . . earthquake . . . woman alone on an island.

Pasiphae *throws* **Ariadne** *at* **Theseus**.

Theseus
Dear queen, apologies I strew them at your feet
Like flowers. But I must take home my trophy.
I need some proof that I have done the deed.
I must cut off the Minotaur's head.

Pasiphae *flies at him, scratching his face with her nails.*

Pasiphae
You bastard! How dare you rub salt into
The wounds of my defeat.
Trying to turn my mourning
Into a bloodbath just for your glorification.
Proof? Proof? They'll know soon enough.
The deed is done.
Have pity Athenian, he is my own-born son.

Theseus *takes the labrys and cuts off the head.* **Pasiphae** *breaks down sobbing on the ground.*

Theseus
His head shall be placed in Poseidon's temple in Athens.
It is necessary.
It is what must be done.

Ariadne
Mother, I . . .

Pasiphae's *wails make all words meaningless.* **Theseus** *holds up the bull's head. Blood pouring everywhere.* **Theseus** *leaves the labrys beside the sobbing* **Pasiphae**. **Ariadne** *winds up the string and* **Theseus** *follows her, blood dripping on the red string.* **Pasiphae** *wails in grief for the Minotaur.*

Scene Six

Ariadne *and* **Theseus** *enter the dungeon where the* **Chorus** *sleeps. They shut the door and* **Ariadne** *locks it. They are both breathless.* **Theseus** *sinks to the ground, staring at the Minotaur's head.*

Ariadne
We'd better wake them and escape . . .

Theseus
Wait . . .

Ariadne
My mother's wails will wake up the palace guard.

Theseus
I need time with my god.

Ariadne
There's no time for that now.
When the ship is sailing, then . . .

Theseus
Please, be quiet.

Ariadne
Put down that head.
That is my brother's head.
My father, if he finds me,
He will kill me.

Theseus
Hush now, or you will call the palace guard.
He will tell me how to go.

Ariadne *falls down sobbing on the pile of clothes where* **Theseus** *slept earlier.*
Theseus *turns his back and, staring into the dead Minotaur's eyes, licks his fingers of the blood and licks his lips thoughtfully.*

Ariadne
I hate you.
You promised you'd take me with you!
You bastard!

Her screams wake the **Chorus**, *bleary-eyed and confused.* **Theseus** *holds her down by her wrists and kisses her to stop her screaming.*

Theseus
I will take you with me.
Now I know you're shocked.
Your brother is dead.
But death makes way for the new

And if the new life that's our future
Is to survive you must remember who you are.
A goddess and a priestess
A lady and a princess
Who has changed sides quite suddenly
In the bloody game of life.
Of course you're scared, but trust me.
I have a channel through to a god
Whose purpose is to save us.
He will if we let him,
Guide and serve us.

By now the Chorus are all fully awake.

Prepare now for escape
But keep quiet and have respect.
Poseidon bides his time.
We are his chosen, his elect.
We go at the moment
Just before the rumbles start.
And if you keep calm
I'll feel them first within my heart.

Ariadne
If he has a heart.
That's debatable.

The **Chorus** *look at the Minotaur's head with a mixture of disgust and awe. They avoid* **Ariadne***'s eyes and say nothing. Some dress or put on shoes, silently.* **Theseus** *kneels, puts his palms flat on the floor, rests his ear against the ground, shuts his eyes and waits. As they are ready, the chorus all do the same until they are all in a circle or a shape reminiscent of the dance ealier. Only* **Ariadne** *does not join them but looks nervously at the door and handles the key wondering what to do. She is rooted to the spot.*

Theseus *stands up, picks up the Minotaur's head and his sword. All the* **Chorus** *stand up. No one has anything to pick up. Silently* **Ariadne** *walks towards the door and unlocks it. They all leave stealthily on tiptoe in a movement reminiscent of their dance. The last one is* **Theseus** *and he locks the door and pockets the key.*

Act Three

Scene One

The **Chorus**, **Theseus** *and* **Ariadne** *all go on board the ship with black sails and as they do the palace and town begin to crumble. A storm at sea.*

Chorus
We'll all be drowned at this rate,
Buoyed up on a tidal wave.
Look at the town shake.
The palace walls shiver as if with cold.
Let's get away from here
Before we're rained on by flying rocks.
Nothing here is safe.
Quick, let's make a quick escape
And trust our luck to the sea.

Theseus
Stop. I've got to get a ring,
Lurking in the bottom of the harbour.

Ariadne
No, leave it, my love,
My queenship here
Means nothing now.
My fate lies with you.

Theseus
I promised I'd get back that ring
And I will keep that promise.

Ariadne
You put us all at risk.

Theseus
Sail on. I'll catch you up.

Theseus *dives over the edge of the ship.*

Chorus
He wants that ring for future possibilities.
Thinking of extending his power to Crete
When the dust has settled.
It's impossible to keep this ship still.
The sea has a life of its own.
He's sure to get thrown against the harbour side.

The ring was right next to it, wasn't it?
That's where he threw it, but who knows
Where it'll be by now?

Ariadne
I've put myself in the hands of a madman.
Suicidal rather than heroic.
There are limits,
Time to draw the line.
He seems to have no sense of that.
Indeed no sense at all.

Chorus
Where is he? All is dark and crashing.
All is out of control.
We'll be down there with him soon.
If we can't get this boat upright.

Ariadne
We've lost. I've lost. Lost.
Family, love, hope, nothing left.
All lost.

Theseus *climbs out of the water, bedraggled and gasping.*

Theseus
Head away from this cursed isle.
Head for home.
There's a presiding wind
From the south-west
That will take us away from all this.
In amongst the crazy confusion
There's hope for us.
Let's use it while we can.
Trim those dark dishevelled sails.

Chorus
Have you got the ring?

Theseus *holds up his hand to show it. They all pull on the ropes of the sails to take advantage of the presiding wind.* **Ariadne** *is the only one who doesn't help. She kneels down and looks at the Minotaur's head.*

Ariadne
That earthquake.
This storm.
Did he predict them?
Did he feel the shake
Before it came
Or did he cause it?

Did he bid me be quiet
While he brewed up
Such a curse?
Did he start the ball rolling
When he dedicated you to
Poseidon, earth-shaker,
Storm-maker?
Does he hate Crete so much
That he must destroy our
Whole world and all who live in it
As well as you?
Yes, he does.
And me, what does he want of me?
Will he give me that ring?
We shall see.

She wraps the Minotaur's head gently in some white sails folded in the hold.

Chorus
For all the fury of the night.
For all the danger of the deep
We seem to be breaking through.
The waves are parting for us,
Uncannily to let us through.
Let's go with it while we can.

Theseus *walks towards* **Ariadne**

Theseus
We made it.

Ariadne
So far.

Theseus
We'll have to stop off somewhere for supplies.

Ariadne
My mother will be crushed
By the earthquake
That you brewed up
Out of the core of the earth
And the depths of the sea.

Theseus
It's your guilt talking.

Ariadne
Guilt?

Theseus
For leaving her. It's natural.
But if you'd stayed
You would have been crushed too.
I needed you, my love.

Ariadne
Needed?

Theseus
And so, too, I will when we go to Athens.
We'll show 'em.
The power of you and I together.
Already we have done so much.
Achieved the impossible.
I couldn't have done it
Without you, guiding.
Near you, now, I can feel your strength.

They embrace.

Ariadne
It's hard for me.
I've lost everything
And gained you.
So, it's hard for me to . . .
I don't know . . .
To treat you fairly,
For you must make up
For so much, so much,
And I know, I suppose,
That that's not even
Possible, not even fair,
At all, to ask so much,
Of one man.

Theseus
One man with a god breathing
Guiding me on my way.
He brought me you.
We're steady set for Naxos.

Chorus
There we'll eat and pick up
Fresh water.
Then we'll stretch out on land
Beneath safe stars.
We'll drink wine
And celebrate the fact we've

Made the impossible come true.
Then we'll take stock
And breathe free,
Before we head for Athens
And the festivals at home.
The celebrating there
Will be heroic mayhem
Tears and hugs and praises all the way.

Scene Two

Chorus, **Theseus** *and* **Ariadne** *on Naxos. They drink and laugh and flirt. They play music sitting or standing around a fire.*

Chorus
All is well. Escape achieved,
And even Ariadne smiles
Once in a while
Now she's on dry land again,
Away from the head of the beast
Wrapped around with blood on the sheet.
Sail.
Same difference.

The music becomes more rhythmic and some start to dance. They pass round the wine.

Theseus
Come dance with me, my sweet,
I know you can.

Ariadne
I've only ever danced for snakes.
Are there snakes in Athens?

Theseus
Why, of course. You have seen my sword.
Snakes are honoured there.
You shall have some if you want them.

Ariadne
I may do. I'll have to see what it's like first.

Theseus
Show me how you dance
The snake dance.

Ariadne *gets up slowly, giggles and, slightly drunk, does the snake dance. The* **Chorus** *and* **Theseus** *form a shape around her, watching, playing music, and gently dancing too. At the end she falls into* **Theseus***'s arms. They kiss and dance together. They perform* *the sexual act as a dance. They fall down, exhausted, and sleep by the dying embers of the fire.*

Scene Three

Fade up on sleeping **Chorus**, **Ariadne** *and* **Theseus** *wound round each other.* **Theseus** *twitching in his sleep, suggesting a dream.* **Theseus** *wakes up, disentangles himself from* **Ariadne**. *He moves among the sleeping bodies and touches them lightly on the shoulder. As he does, each wakes and he beckons them. Confused, hungover, but silent, they tiptoe away from the sleeping* **Ariadne**. *They get on the boat and cast away.* **Ariadne** *reaches out for* **Theseus** *in her sleep. Wakes up, looks around and realizes she's been deserted amongst the debris of last night's drinking bout.*

Ariadne
Aphrodite, goddess of love,
You bitch!
You filled me up with false hope
The lust of love and the love of lust
From the depths of my womb
To the sparkling surface of my eyes
You set me alight
With a desire irresistable for my enemy
Some bastard upstart Athenian prince
Full of fire
Warming every cell in my body
Full of air
Lightening my every thought
Full of earth grounding me with desire to be grounded
Full of water
Crashing, flowing, filling up every space within me.
All that for this,
To be abandoned on a deserted shore
For love I turned against my own father
My own mother
Daughter turned traitor
Princess turned spy
A curse on you, Theseus
And on all your family worse.
On all Athens I lay my curse,
On all men. I warn women
All women alive and yet to live
Do not give
Do not give freely of your love.
Beware!
In love you're in a minefield.

The man closest to your heart
May be a stranger.
Should the fancy take,
The moment turn,
Some vision of female beauty
Other than your own
Or political machination
Of which you are not aware
Maybe clicking in that power-crazed
Machine he calls his brain.
Beware!
His heart may be flowering
Yet his mind can deaden by decision
Love within the hour.
Do not believe the whispers of the night
Brought on by lust
Or sipping too much wine.
Do not trust for trusting him you make yourself the fool.
May my warning echo over the sea
And down the ages yet to come.
Give not your heart,
But hold on to your head.
Scheme, practice deception,
Do what you will, but banish
Honesty, purity, love.
Hide behind the mask and let not
Aphrodite have her wicked way.
For she will overturn reason, upset inner balance.
Banish her and all her wiles
Don't give into the pretence of men's smiles
But rule yourself,
Don't let some goddess hold sway
However powerful she may be.

Scene Four

Theseus *stares out to sea and* **Chorus** *sit around on deck, plaiting each other's hair and playing 'Knife, Papyrus, Stone'*

Chorus
As we sail north
It feels more and more like home.
And not having Ariadne here.
She brought the perfume of Crete with her.
Theseus is quiet.

He hasn't said a word to me.
He's brooding, but all that will change
When he's home and sees his father
Once again.
I can't wait to see my mother.
I long to be in my loved ones' arms again.
They'll be harvesting the grapes.
What a time to arrive.
Feasts and parades already planned.
The wine running free
And much thanking of the gods.
Poseidon waits for the bull-man's head.
It will be displayed on his altar
For all to see.
I can't wait for that first glimpse
Of Athens' shore.
The shouts of rejoice.
The people swarming to the harbour side.
The tears of joy
Shed in utter disbelief.
Feeling our families near.
It's all down to Theseus,
But there's no talking to him.
There's no thanking him.
He looks out to sea
Like one who's lost.
Better leave him alone.
Better leave him to heal inside.
Better leave him be.
Yes, you're right, I'm sure.
But it hurts me to see him
Who should be feeling so full of himself.
He looks so low.
Till the next fight, the next storm,
The wind is out of his sails
And there's no fight to fight.
Yes, maybe, you're right.

Scene Five

Aegeus *sits on the cliff-top in Athens, looking out to sea in a manner reminiscent of* **Theseus** *in the last scene.*

Aegeus
The grape is ripe

And most are gathered in.
The people sing and dance
Along our streets
For joy.
Helped of course by the
Flowing of good wine.
I smile down upon them
Yet I'm desolate inside.
So long I waited for my son.
And when at last I had him
By my side,
When I realised he was a hero
Through and through,
Then he was gone.
A sacrifice too great.
A pain too sharp to bear.
I've looked out to sea
Till blobs of light
Float before my eyes.
Squinting out to sea.
Praying to the gods
For white sails.
The hope is foolish.
An old man grasping on to straws.
Staggering from oracle to oracle,
When the night means
I can no longer
Keep watch out to sea.
Entrails, ashes, the paths that snakes
Make in the sand,
The way bones fall
Scattered on the dusty ground.
I who am king,
Reduced to this.
What's this?
A black-sailed boat
Near the horizon
A speck against the almost setting sun.
Is this illusion or real?

He wipes his eyes and finds he is crying.

Black sails can only mean one thing.
No, it is the boat returned
Without him.
He who is my heir,
My hope, my hero and my son.

I'm left stranded on the end of
The line of kings.
Fate!
I cannot face the red-faced sailors
Telling me the gory details.
I cannot face the people
Looking down to hide
The pity in their eyes.
I cannot face the sons of Pallas
Keen to divide and thus destroy
All that I have built up.
I cannot face those black sails.
Blot out, go, go, go.
Let go.
Poseidon, take me.
Save me from facing
One more moment of
My fated life.

He throws himself off the cliff.

Scene Six

The ship arrives in the harbour in Athens. The **Chorus** *rush off excitedly.* **Theseus**
picks up the Minotaur's head in the bloody sail. He takes it to Poseidon's temple. He
places it on the altar in the temple and opens out the sail. He kneels down and bows,
palms flat on the floor. One of the **Chorus** *enters the sanctuary.*

Chorus
I do not want to disturb you
In your moment of offering
The beast up to your god,
But there is news I know
You need to hear and so
I came straight to you.

Theseus
So? What is it?

Chorus
It's your father, Theseus.
He's dead.
He threw himself off the cliff.
He was keeping watch.
He must have given up.

Theseus
And now? Where is his body now?

Chorus
They fished him out.
He's on a slab of rock
Down by the sea.

Theseus
Bring him to me.
But first leave me alone, one moment.

Chorus exits. **Theseus** kneels, palms on floor.

Theseus
Thank you, father.
Thank you.
You've taken him into your sea
And left the rule of Athens to me.

Chorus bring on body of **Aegeus** and place it on black sail.

Theseus
Father, I will be worthy of you.
I will.
I may be a bastard
But I will be king.
I'm ambitious.

Theseus takes the crown off **Aegeus**'s head.

Yes, but ambitious to do good.
I'll pull together warring states.
I'll see islanders and mainlanders
Pull together in my name.
The people will love me.
They'll want me all right.
And they'll be right.
I'm the best man for the job.
They'll need me
Even if they don't yet know it.
By the time I've finished,
They'll know it all right.
They'll know it.
No risk too great.
No task too arduous.
No fear I won't face.
For Athens I will do it.
For my people I will do it.
For the world I will do it.
I will. I will. I will.

Theseus crowns himself.

The Labyrinth That Is In All Of Us

Jan Maloney interviewed by Jim Mulligan

With a steady output of a play a year and regular workshops, Jan Maloney is kept busy writing. She was 'a bit of a rebel' at her South London comprehensive and walked out without taking A Levels. She later scraped through enough A Levels for her to combine the bringing up of two children with studying for a degree. In between, she had been a performer on the London Fringe for five years, and had been writing consistently including sketches, lyrics, poetry, stories and plays.

'I tend to use poetic or heightened language in all my writing. I am extremely fond of strong images and ritual. *The Minotaur* particularly lends itself to this kind of writing. The story comes from Ovid's *Metamorphoses* and is such a dramatic story I was certain there must have been a play about it, but none has ever been found, so I decided to write as if I were giving a modern translation of an ancient play. I wrote in blank verse with a Chorus and main characters. The minute we step into the world of ancient Athens or Crete we are in a rich symbolic landscape, and although the language is heightened, I have tried to make it colloquial and relaxed. And occasionally I use anachronisms to make the audience laugh, but essentially to give them a little jolt and remind them that we are in the world today.'

Before writing the play, Jan Maloney immersed herself in the Minotaur myth, relying heavily on original sources and Robert Graves. She assumed that most people would have a vague idea of the story about the Minotaur – half-bull, half-man, incarcerated in a maze – but she assumed nothing more. She lets the play tell the story and slips in details of the conflict between Athens and Crete and the mythology that underpinned Greek culture. 'You can go to Knossos in Crete today and buy snake goddess figurines, portraying a woman with naked breasts holding a snake in each hand. The mythology is rooted in the axis between the two astrological signs, Taurus and Scorpio. If you lived on an island like Crete, surrounded by sea, you would give great importance to Poseidon, the god of the sea and earthquakes. The Minotaur is half-man and half-bull and I wanted to explore the sexuality of that. When you're growing up, you feel intensely that you are more than just a human being, that you are more than you are expected to be or can be. So I have made *The Minotaur* a coming-of-age play, where the participants can come to terms with their fears, or what they perceive as the negative parts of themselves.'

There are clearly distinct voices dwelling within the Chorus, a fact which gives directors the flexibility to divide it up as they wish. But the Chorus is also the voice of the ordinary people who are onlookers and commentators. And yet the people of the Chorus are in a very specific situation, almost as if they were prisoners of war.

'One of the reasons I am pleased with the play is that it works on many different levels. You can see Athens and Crete as a labyrinth beneath whose calm surface all is rotting. And you could apply it to our society, which is manifestly covered in rotting debris. But I was not making a comment about Britain in the 1990s. This play is relevant to the inner psyche, and so of course it is relevant to today, but because it is a myth, it transcends our political problems, important though they are.'

The Minotaur is often perceived as a monster, imprisoned and kept out of sight, but Jan Maloney does not see any monsters in her play. The Minotaur is portrayed as a brother who is loved and protected by his half-sister. Nor are the people who imprisoned him monsters to her. They are all caught up in the power sruggle between Athens and Crete. It might appear that Theseus has a problem: do I kill the half-brother of the woman I love, or do I let my companions perish? But for Jan Maloney, there is only one way he can go.'It was never in doubt that Theseus would kill the Minotaur. That was a problem that had to be overcome in order for him to get where he is going. Nor is there any question of his bringing back Ariadne with him. She was one of the enemy, and his career would have been finished if he had married her. He uses her and she doesn't fully trust him, but there is nothing either of them can do. This is a power-struggle.'

The dramatic question central to the play is why Theseus chose to return with black sails when he knew what the consequences would be. It is an unresolved question. Someone had used the white sails to wrap up the Minotaur's head and they were stained with blood, so in that sense they were not available. Nonetheless, Theseus could have ordered white sails to be used. It is dramatically possible that if the sailors had started to unfurl the white sails, Theseus would have allowed them to continue. 'It is one of those things you will never know, just as you will never know if Theseus loved Ariadne. What is certain is that this is a play about power and sexuality. The play throbs with it, especially when they are on the boat, aching to have sex, but must remain virgins – although two of them do give in to it. It is also about the labyrinth that is in all of us. In my play the altar, covered in guts, is the shape of the labyrinth, which in turn is the shape of the womb, or convoluted like the brain, or as intricately folded as the intestines. You could say the story has something to do with birth, or getting lost in our minds, or feeling things in our guts.'

Jan Maloney's first plays, *Living by the River* and *Sam the Man*, were performed at the Green Room in Manchester. Her next play, *Cherub*, has been performed nationally at various venues including the Contact Theatre, Manchester, and the Man in the Moon Theatre, London. It was also shortlisted for the Verity Bargate Award in 1989. In 1990, *Cristabella and the Cabbage Seller* was performed as part of 'New Writing North' at the Live Theatre, Newcastle. Most recently she was commissioned by Gay Sweatshop and wrote *In Your Face*, which toured in the UK and went to New York. An earlier version of *The Minotaur* was performed at the Contact Theatre, Manchester, in 1992.

The Minotaur

Production Notes

Setting and staging

Jan Maloney has created a dramatization where both Athens and Crete suggest an image of 'a labyrinth beneath whose calm all is rotting'. Although this comment could be applied to our society, it would be a mistake to give the play a specific contemporary setting. Rather let the audience draw meanings from the story as it unfolds.

This is an ensemble piece of physical theatre. The chorus will need to help suggest the following: a harbour, beside which lies a ship with black sails; a snake pit; a dungeon; the cliff tops of Athens; a labyrinth; and a ship with moving sails. The Minotaur might be suggested through the use of a shadow puppet and a fully masked figure. His head will need to be produced, dripping with blood; likewise his guts, three times the size of the humans' guts he ate earlier, again dripping with blood. (Whether the company will try to create a 'literal' blood effect, or indicate it theatrically using lighting, strips of fabric, etc., is their choice).

Sound is crucial, in suggesting the lapping of water at the dock, a storm at sea, an earthquake. The play might benefit from the use of live music.

There is much reliance on **movement** to create the ship, the labyrinth, various dances. The chorus will need to work closely together when, for instance, they react to the tremors created by the Minotaur, or when they discover their 'land legs'.

Costumes

Principal characters might stand out if costumed in different colours from the Chorus (who might be masked, provided the masks allow clarity of voice). Theseus needs a lion skin at one point; he carries a sword, and takes the crown from Aegeus. This play provides opportunities for groups to explore Minoan/Mycenean costume, masks, etc. (NB not classical Greece). It might be worth following up the notion that the modern Spanish bullfight is descended from the Cretan 'bull dance'.

Casting

Besides the Chorus of fourteen, each of whom has an individual speaking role, there are Theseus, Ariadne, Aegeus, Minos, Pasiphae and the Minotaur. It would be useful if some of the chorus could also play musical instruments.

Questions

1. Why are Athens and Crete in conflict?

2. Who is the Minotaur?

3. Why is he imprisoned?

4. Why does Theseus kill the Minotaur? What are his motives?

5. Why does Theseus return to Athens with black sails? How does he feel as he approaches Piraeus?

6. 'There is a labyrinth in all of us'. Do you agree? If so, describe your personal labyrinth.

7. What role has Daedalus had in setting up the situation?

8. How would you define a hero? Is Theseus one?

9. Which characters suffer betrayal and why?

10. What role do the gods play in the piece?

Exercises

1. The Chorus. The chorus is the voice of the people, and comments on the story as it unfolds. It is useful to ask the same questions of the chorus as you would of any other character. How are they affected by events? For instance, when Theseus throws the ring into the sea, they say:

> Please calm down
> You put our lives on the line
> When you throw yourself recklessly against his will.

Since they are a group, rather than a sole individual, how does their 'synchronized' behaviour come about? (Football-crowd chants might be an interesting area for research).

2. Various settings need to be suggested by the chorus. For example, the use of a dark sheet and ropes to suggest the ship, or the snake pit. NB The Parachute Game is useful in helping the group to 'brainstorm' ideas and in creating a working ensemble. It is best to find your own way of experimenting with a 'parachute', but here are a few suggestions.

   i   In a large space, have the group evenly distributed around the parachute, extending it as tautly as possible at waist level. At a pre-arranged signal, the group throws the parachute in the air as high as possible, and each member swaps places with another across the circle in time to catch the parachute on its descent.

   ii Repeat the above exercise, with half of the group remaining stationary to catch the parachute. The other half will be free to create a series of different tableaux from the play, within the circle, in the space of time it takes the parachute to descend. With practice, the group can alternate.

   iii Use the parachute to suggest sails billowing, a crow's wing, a funeral cloth. Have Theseus use it as a cloak with the chorus fanning it out as he walks around the space. Discover what dramatic effects you can get and what they say about Theseus' status. (Experiment by perhaps giving him a neutral mask, and asking him to move in an appropriate way). Add music and/or sound to any of the above.

iv Take a choral section, e.g. the one in Act III, Scene 4. Cut up the speech into about twenty pieces and number them chronologically, duplicating, say, five. Place the numbered pieces of paper in the middle of a circle. As a group, pick up one or more pieces of paper at random. Count through numbers one to twenty and memorise which member of the group holds the number before yours. Read your line[s] for understanding, and then experiment with ways of expressing the meaning. Come together as a chorus in the circle and work through the section, listening to the effect more than one voice can have on the lines that are duplicated. Memorize the lines, and as a group, walk around the space, repeating them. Work through the section collectively, telling the story as clearly as possible. Avoid being over-reverential with the poetical language.

3. Be clear about the various characters' histories. Design a family tree for Ariadne and Theseus.

Suzy Graham-Adriani
Director/Producer for BT National Connections

The Bedbug

Snoo Wilson

(adapted from the play by Vladimir Mayakovsky)

Characters

Ivan Varlet	Or, Ivor Violet. Former Party member, former worker, now the fiancé of
Elzevir Davidovna Bornagin	Manicurist and cashier of a beauty parlour.
Rosalie Pavlovna Bornagin	her mother.
David Sofagherkin Bornagin	her father
Zoya Byrioshka	A working girl.
Oleg Bard	An eccentric house-owner

Police
Professor
Zoo director
Fire Chief
Usher
Reporters
Workers' Chairman of City Soviet
Orator
High school students
Master of Ceremonies
Members of Presidium of City Soviet
Hunters
Children
Old People.

Scene One

A backdrop of a colourless and glum Russian state department store. All the action takes place outside on the street. The cries of the street vendors all overlaid, in a scene-setting panorama.

Button-seller – Comrades, the humble trouserbutton performs an essential function in our socialist paradise. It holds the male trouser up. But what are better than buttons? The answer is – Dutch press studs. I'll tell you why in just a moment –

Doll-seller – Dancing dolls, dancing dolls, light as a feather, ready and willing in all kinds of weather (*Music. Demonstrates.*) Have your own little ballerina in your very own home –

Button-seller I'm selling twenty-four hour control here! You've never had it so good –

Woman selling bananas – No kiwis, no melons. But good socialist bananas! Today as a special offer to heroic female members of the party, who might be short of demonstrations of comradely affection – I'm not asking twenty, I'm not asking eighteen, they're fifteen kopecks apiece, to you, ladies. The bargain bananas are yours for the gobbling. Put the best Russian manhood to shame, these would!

Lampshade-seller Lampshades here, for every occasion. Blushing blue for considering proposals under, in the comrades' lounge, then later, when dalliance arises, how about this red one for the modern bedroom –

Balloon-seller *is making up animals with long thin balloons.*

Balloon-seller What am I doing? I'll tell you. With these all-socialist balloons at five kopecks, you can make animals – see – like a sweet little post-monarchist sausage dog – you try.

He gives an untied balloon to a small boy. Boy lets go and balloon deflates.

Balloon-seller You got to hold on tight to its arse. Have another try now. Thing is, even with with socialist balloons it all whooshes out – That's right – whoops – (*Balloon flies out of boy's hand again.*)

Herring-seller Herrings! Non-Tsarist herrings! Republican Herrings!

Bra-seller – Lovely brassières, trimmed with mink. Ladies, you never seen anything like them in Rome or Paris. Not just thermal – decorative too –

Bookseller – Books, books. 'How to' books on all subjects. This one – special offer – How to commit adultery – a spicy ribtickler by ex-Count Leo Tolstoy, full of practical hints –

Bra-seller   Thermal brassières trimmed with mink! All sizes!

Enter **Varlet** *and his mother-in-law,* **Rosalie Pavlovna***, and* **Oleg***.*

Varlet   I say, look at these aristocratic nightcaps! Is it real fur?

Varlet *puts a bra from a stall on his head.*

Bra seller   Real? Is this lovely fur *real*? Was Cleopatra a snake fancier? Feel that silkiness. It's from the inside legs of the animals. But there wasn't no suffering involved. These little minks were sleeping on silk, crammed with cream, before they finally sacrificed themselves for the people.

Rosalie   Comrade Violet, I wouldn't advise trying to put your head in one of those. There are two, see?

Varlet   Away with you, foolish creature. I always have two of everything that catches my fancy.

Rosalie   But they're not for your sort. They're for supporting parts of outstanding female party members.

Varlet   What nonsense. After I marry your daughter Elzevir, these trinkets will dress what comes to pass.

Rosalie   Get away! You're not one of them cross-dressers are you? And I thought he was an honest prole, not a decadent capitalist!

Varlet   I'm talking exactly nine months after. I know they will make superior hats for your future grandchildren. They can put them on when they go out together in the park.

Rosalie   Siamese twins, they'll have to be.

Varlet   We'll have twins, naturally – because I am going to have two of everything I want in the future. It is written!

Oleg   I think what Ivor Violet here, his Working-Classness, is doing is bringing an innocent proletarian eye to bear on everyday creations, and transforming their use-value with his incisive intelligence, don't you?

Rosalie   I didn't realize that union with the proletariat meant that my grandchildren will have to go round forever with their heads crammed into one fur-trimmed brassière.

Oleg   Rosalie, don't provoke his Working-Classness – don't forget, with your kind of background, you need to get that union card in your front room.

Doll-seller   (*background*) – Dancing dolls, dancing dolls, light as a feather, ready and willing in all kinds of weather –

Oleg   If he wants two of everything, it's his by right! He's the man of the hour!

Varlet (*to* **Doll-seller**) Hither, fellow. (*Examines dolls.*) 'The fruit of the proletarian loom must be able to step out of its cradling, into culture and elegance.'

Rosalie You'd better have two of them, too.

Varlet No. I don't just want two, I want a regiment of those.

Rosalie But Comrade Violet!

Varlet Don't 'Comrade' me till your family's officially united with the one true class, the proles. That won't be till after the marriage. For now, you are still bourgeoise, so watch what you say.

Rosalie I take your point, Future Comrade Violet, but for the money we're spending, we could smarten up any number of your compatriots – shave and shampoo a dozen of the grottiest proles – if the wedding's going to go off with a bang, we're going to need to budget for some booze.

Varlet Do you imagine I can have forgotten drink? Of course not.

Oleg That's right! The wedding is the union of the classes in peace and harmony. Beer will rain down as if the bottom had fallen out of Valhalla. You'll be swimming in it, with vodka chasers to keep your strength up. Don't upset him now Rosalie! His is the class of the future. The bourgeois class, it is written, are mere mushrooms which spring up in the night and then wither and are heard of no more. Think of it this way. The trousers of future Comrade Violet, however repellent, contain within them the socialist horn-of-plenty!

Herring-man Finest post-Tzarist herrings! Essential accompaniment to all kinds of vodka!

Rosalie (*brightening*) You hear that? Salted herrings are the very thing for a wedding! Out of my way, young prole-gentleman. (*Looking.*) Oh dear, how disappointing.

Oleg Let me carry them – I won't charge a penny –

Rosalie How much do you want to get rid of these horrid little stunted sardines?

Herring-man I can't let these salmon go at under two roubles sixty. They weigh a full kilo each.

Rosalie Two-sixty for a piddling minnow like that?

Herring-man That's no minnow, that's an apprentice sturgeon! Look at the fat on those gills!

Rosalie Sturgeon? More like a twiglet fish. Well I'm not standing here arguing, we've had a revolution in case you haven't heard. I'm going to get some decent fish from the Soviet State Co-op! (*Exits.*)

Oleg   Oh this is all so unnecessary. Future Comrade Violet, why let your dear future mother-in-law get involved in tasteless street polemics, when for fifteen roubles and a bottle of vodka I can personally guarantee the best wedding that you'll ever have in your life?

Varlet   Others are going to be handling the petty-bourgeois details. I don't care to be involved.

Oleg   Alright, then have you thought of having your nuptials conducted along the lines of the ancient Rites of Eleusis? Eleusis of the ancient world, the fountain of our culture, where sacred drama and religion both drank from the same stream? We can reconstruct the rites for your ceremony. When the wedding procession advances, holding sheaves of corn in front of the bride, I will sing in praise of Hymen.

Varlet   Hymen? Hymen who?

Oleg   Hymen's the ancient goddess of marriage and fertility.

Varlet   No no. I want an honest-to-goodness Red wedding, with no decadent foreign trimmings, like – people without patronymics.

Oleg   Of course, I see now that the wedding has to obey our Russian dramatic unities – I refer to the coming unities, of class . . . let's see . . . a Red . . . we envision the red-dressed Red wife-to-be stepping out of her carriage as she arrives on the arm of the red accountant, the universal proxy father-in-law, representing the state, she's looking pretty steamed-up, but he's ooh, red as a beetroot. And then the Red red groom is ushered in by the Red ushers, and the red tablecloth is covered with bowls of steaming borscht and juicy red hams. How does that envision for a start?

Violet   Oh, just the ticket!

Enter **Zoya**. *She circles them suspiciously.*

Oleg   Then the blushing guests tear the red, red tops off the vodka bottles with sweaty fingers and pour the proper vodka down their red throats, and when they look down at you again to draw breath, they shout, 'Kiss, kiss!' and your brand-new encarminated red-hot spouse with her tongue weaving like a red cobra inside her mouth comes towards you closer and closer till her panting embouchure closes succulently on your own rosy face sphincter, sploosh! – recipe for mutual rapture.

Zoya   Just a minute. Ivan! What's this old cow going on about? What wedding? Who's getting married?

Varlet   Nothing's happened yet, Zoya. But I do not, I cannot know you any more.

Zoya   Why not? What are you two talking about?

Oleg The future rubicund nuptials, I am assisting in arranging, between Elzevir Davidovna Bornagin, and this eminent prole-gentleman here. Ivor Violet.

Zoya His name is Ivan Varlet, and he was engaged to me! What's going on Ivan?

Varlet (*sings*) I'M SORRY THIS HAS COME TO PASS, OH MY ZOYA
IT'S NOT A MATTER OF HER TITS AND ARSE.
I'M MARRYING A DIFFERENT CLASS, THEY'RE
CALLED EMPLOYERS.

Zoya What about me, Ivan?

Varlet Ivan? Who he? Ivan exists only in memory. Enter Ivor, the new man!

Zoya You're not that different.

Varlet I am too! Ivan drank like a fish. He had a drunken way with him, and his guitar, his life was understandably short. He's gone, I have disinvented him.

Zoya Ivan Varlet! You said you and me belonged together like pork and beans!

Varlet You might have belonged to Ivan, true. A woman in every smokey bar, a chicken in every port. But you are are well rid of him. Do not weep, I have become the manifest destiny of my class.

Zoya Ivan – you once said our hearts beat as one. And that we would work for the good of our class together forever. Don't tell me it's over, Ivan.

Varlet It's over. The iron tongue of determinism has chimed midnight, and I declare our love liquidated, citizen. I shall summon the people's trusty law enforcers if you try to obstruct my heart's new direction with your plebeian fisticuffs. All that is behind me.

Re-enter **Rosalie**.

Rosalie And the fish I saw in there are even smaller . . . (*Sees* **Zoya**.) Just a minute, what's going on. Who's this little slut?

Rosalie *starts to knock* **Zoya** *around. A crowd gathers, cheering as they whack at each other with their handbags.*

Zoya Piss off! Who are you?

Rosalie Has she got her hooks into you, future comrade Ivor? Piss off yerself, you little tart, he's going to be my son-in-law!

Zoya His fate is tied to mine. Irreversibly.

Rosalie   Aha! You mean you're pregnant and you want money. Alright fair's fair, I'll pay you off here and now.

Zoya   You lot can only think of money!

Rosalie   Not true! When I've paid you off I'm going to split your nostril into the bargain, you little slut. Come here!

Police   (*sings*) CITIZENS! PLEASE STOP THIS UGLY SCENE
ADMIT THE LAW MUST THROW ITSELF BETWEEEN
ALL DISPUTES IN SOCIALIST PARADISE
WE'RE THE POLICE, WE DON'T ASK TWICE
WE ARREST EVERY ACTION UNDERHAND
AND IF YOU'RE DRUNK WE'LL PUT YOU IN THE
CAN –
CITIZENS! PLEASE STOP THIS UGLY SCENE

Etc, and fade over scene change.

Scene Two

Grotty Hostel with dirty bunks, for young workers. **Inventor**, **Cleaner**, **Barefoot youth**, **Girl** *in spectacles.* **Barefoot youth** *screams and runs around.*

Barefoot youth   Oi! Me grass shoots!

Girl   Yer wot?

Barefoot youth   Some capitalist swine's nicked me daisy roots again! The last time, I tried to leave 'em in hand luggage at the railway station, last thing, but they won't take anything smelling that ripe. What am I supposed to do, sleep with the effing cheesers on?

Cleaner   I meant to tell you. Ivan Varlet's borrowed them to see that bourgeois cow he's going to get hitched with. *He* was effing and blinding trying to get them on.

Barefoot youth   I bet he split 'em, the poxy class traitor!

Cleaner   I bet his language will improve faster than yours, though. He did say he was never going to have to use the effski word again, now he's moving up the social ladder!

Barefoot youth   All this crap he's leaving round – it's not like it used to be. Before it was old sardine tins and empty beer bottles, now it's bottles of aftershave which came in this amazingly poncy wrapping paper. Changed his name, too, I hear. Effing *ponce*.

Cleaner   Now, now, stop that or the warden'll –

Barefoot youth   – Ponce, ponce, that's what all class traitors are.

Girl   Class traitor, arse traitor. Just because he's got a flash new tie an' gear, you're going on like he was an poncing enemy of the people.

Barefoot youth   He *is* a poncy bloody enemy of the people. I'm the people, aren't I? I told him not to take my boots and look what he done. But you know, he's not going to fool anyone into thinking he's not still a prole. He's so thick, when he tightens his tie, it'll stop any blood getting to his brain at all.

Inventor   As a matter of fact, he's not so stupid after all – seems to have reinvented himself. Seen this box of calling cards? (*Shows them round.*)

All   Ivor Violet! Wooooo!

Displays of extravagant and contemptuous mirth. **Inventor** *takes bottle of aftershave.*

Barefoot youth   'Ere you, what are you nicking?

Inventor   With his new name, does 'Ivor Violet' even need aftershave? He smells good enough already?

Barefoot youth Leave it mate, it's got class contamination written all over it!

Girl You can mock, but he's changed. He's started a one-man cultural revolution in the domestic sphere, from right here in the hostel!

Barefoot youth And then he had this way of smarming this horrible smelling stuff all over his sideburns. No wonder they call 'em buggers' grips.

Inventor (*surprised*) Was that why they was invented?

Barefoot youth They hang off the side of his face like something nasty off a dog's behind.

Girl Oh shut up, Lotsa movie stars have sideburns now.

Barefoot youth But he's not a movie star. He's a mechanic!

Enter **Greasy Mechanic**

Mechanic Not any more. That's all in the past. Comrade Ivan Varlet came in and chucked his job in today. Said factory work was incompatible with his new wife.

Girl Who is this lucky girl then?

Barefoot youth Not you, obviously.

Girl Piss off!

Mechanic A hairdresser's daughter is what he's landed. Yep. The poodle-fancying class threw him a lure, and they is reeling him in now. I expect she'll sort his side-whiskers out for free and then buff his pinky afterwards till the welkin rings.

Girl Lucky for him. Ivan Varlet's improved himself and you're all jealous! If little miss pinky-buffer waved one of her tits at you, you'd be there like a rat up a drainpipe.

Mechanic I'm not marrying no posh hairdresser. I'm a socialist. We're building a new state, houses for everyone. It's tough. It's war, mate, but that doesn't mean I'm surrendering my principles.

Barefoot youth The war's over. It stopped being 1917 a while back. The revolution's finished, dad! Go and get your hair permed!

Enter **Oleg** *and* **Ivan** *with shiny shoes. He throws the boots to* **Barefoot youth.**,

Oleg – One last lesson and you will be perfect. Head up now – *Meinheer* Ivor, refinement for your new class consists of occasionally ignoring the obvious. Now, follow my instructions. Music ho!

A foxtrot sounds out of a crackling gramophone playing a '78. The hostel boos and blows raspberries.

Oleg At the nuptial climax of our modern wedding, the seductive rhythm of the foxtrot will insinuate itself into the guests' consciousness. And we will all . . . step out onto the dance floor!

Varlet Can I take my shoes off? They're playing old harry with my corns.

Oleg Step up, sir, imagine your bride standing here and one, two, three and off! (**Varlet** *dances by himself*.)

Barefoot youth Class traitor!

Oleg Very nicely sir! Now, Monsignor Violet, the moon is riding high, filling your soul with longing and passion – the night-scented stock fills the air with heavy perfume, and what are you doing? You are weaving dreamily back from a well stocked taverna. The Rites of Eleusis were always concluded with a dance. Don't wiggle your rear end, and you're supposed to be leading your lovely partner, not carrying a sack of spuds. Too high! Watch that hand!

Varlet It won't stay up!

Oleg Alright, well, just locate the lovely lady's brassière, and hook your thumb in it – it makes it easy for you and it's very pleasant for the lady too. Now you can experiment with the other arm. What on earth are you doing with your shoulders?

Ivan*'s dance gets wilder and wilder.*

Oleg That's not a foxtrot. It's something greater! You have a talent and no mistake. You're too big for this country! You should break into Europe and astonish them all! Beyond socialism! The song of the body beautiful! The Moulin Rouge will never be the same after you conquer Paris! More, more! Encore! Bravo!! Magnificent!

Music ends, stopped by **Mechanic**.

Oleg Oh, I'm exhausted already, but I must go and finish off the preparations – if I don't keep the ushers off the booze we'll never get there. Tuck your shirt inside your trousers but not inside the underpants. That is, provided you have underpants. . . .

Oleg *leaves.*

Barefoot youth Oy, dog's dinner! What's going on then?

Varlet Etiquette would say, none of your business, respected Comrade. But I will tell you. I have fought for the good life, and I have won. Furthermore, I'm doing my class, the proletariat, a favour by raising the average standard of living. What do you say to that?

Gunshot, off. Enter **Youth**.

Barefoot youth   'Ere! Ivan Varlet's rejected fiancée's shot herself! You know, Zoya Wasserpatronymic! I don't know how she's going to explain herself at the next Party meeting!

Voices   Help! First aid! Help! First Aid!

Zoya *is carried in by excited pedestrians.*

Man   Missed the heart, thank God – but shot herself right through the tits! Got to phone for assistance!

Mechanic   There's no phone here!

Crowd   (*enthusiastic*) Emergency! Emergency! Emergency! Emergency!

Crowd exits, leaving **Zoya** *on floor.*

Varlet   My past is behind me. Destiny calls. The time has come at last to change classes.

Varlet *steps over* **Zoya** *and comes downstage to hail cab.*

Varlet   Cabbie! Seventeen Lunacharsky street, otherwise known as Hairdresser Hall. Don't forget my baggage!

Varlet   FAREWELL TO POVERTY, LICE AND CHEAP
               PROPAGANDA (*Exiting.*)
               HELLO TO RELAXED SUMMER EVENINGS WITH
               TRIVIAL CHATTER UPON THE VERANDAH –

Exits, leaving **Mechanic** *alone with body of* **Zoya**. **Mechanic** *kneels, weeping, to hold her hand. The crowd comes back and surrounds them. Music.*

Mechanic   Don't die, my love!

Zoya   (*faintly*) To think I tried to kill myself over a greasy worthless jerk like Ivan. There's nothing stupider than misplaced love.

Mechanic   I know what you mean.

Cloth cap off, hand on heart.

Mechanic   (*sings*) WE'VE BEEN BUILDING A BRIDGE TO A
               BETTER WORLD FOR NIGH ON SEVEN YEARS
               BUT I'VE NOTICED SOMETHING WEIRD AND
               SAD.
               I SHOULD HAVE DROPPED A TEAR
               THE BRIDGE TO SOCIALISM LEADS STRAIGHT
               INTO A WALL
               AND THE WALL DON'T WANT US, DON'T WANT
               US
               AT ALL –

Zoya *stands to sing with the* **Mechanic** *and the crowd.*

All HARK TO WHAT OUR MASTERS SAID
SWING YOUR HAMMER, SWING WITH DREAD
HIT THAT RIVET ON THE HEAD
BUT THE DREAM WILL FALL
BUT THE DREAM WILL FALL

Scene Three

Beauty parlour is the site for the Red Wedding. Bottles of vodka as **Oleg** *has promised, and some disgusting-looking food.* **Varlet, Elzevir Bornagin, Best Man, Accountant,** *and* **Matron of Honour,** *Accountant's wife.* **Oleg** *is Master of Ceremonies. On stage an 'ethnic' wedding band, e.g. Georgian, covered in bandoliers, with huge handlebar moustaches and balalaikas, to taste.*

Elzevir   I think we could start, Ivor darling, don't you?

Varlet   Not so fast!

Elzevir   What's the matter? Don't you want to get married after all?

Varlet   You bourgies have a thing or two to learn about protocol in this new world! On these important occasions of inter-class mingling, protocol has to be strictly observed. In addition to the Best Man, the Accountant, and Matron of Honour, his regularly-fulfilled wife, the secretary of the committee of our glorious steering-wheel factory has graciously accepted our invitation. And look where he comes!

Guest runs in.

Elzevir   Oh, is Mr Steering-Wheel the guest of honour? Some sort of super-prole? I see. Alright, very nice.

Varlet   Deigning graciously to illuminate our nupitials with his working-class brilliance, and repartee – the witty and resourceful representative of socialised motor vehicles, Comrade Lassalchenko! (*Pause.*)

Guest   Party greetings and apologies for absence – from Comrade Lassalchenko. His message reads (*Reads.*) 'Tomorrow I can go anywhere – even as far as church. Today, however is a Party day, and like it or lump it, I have to report to my Party Committee in full.' Message ends. (*Exits.*)

Varlet   So that's that. Apologies having been tendered, we should move on to the next item on the agenda.

Opens champage bottle and sprays it over **Elzevir**.

Elzevir   Just a minute – what sort of celebration is this – you're ruining my dress!

Varlet   I hereby declare this wedding – open!

Cheers and the guests rush for the food.

Rosalie   Comrades, proles, nuptial sponsors of the hour from all sexes – please help yourselves from the generous buffet. I've been saving the ham for a rainy day ever since the end of the war. It's impossible to find porkers tasting like they do nowadays. They just don't feed piggies the right food.

A musical interlude where everyone eats furiously.

Best Man   Next item – drink!

All stop eating. Rush to drinks, take and raise bottles.

Best Man   And now, the smooch that proclaims the twin fleshes one inseparable for evermore till divoce do 'em part!

All   Kiss! Kiss! (**Elzevir** *and* **Varlet** *kiss.*) Kiss! Kiss!

Elzevir *kisses* **Varlet** *with passion. He returns kisses stolidly.*

Best Man   We witness here the historic embrace of the broad masses, by the bourgeois! C'mon, let's hot it up! We Russians know how to celebrate – We celebrate Shakespeare's birthday – an' Beethoven – in fact we celebrate 'em both, all day, every day – so let's get a piano in here – and really make this an outstanding occasion!

Piano is pushed on. **Oleg** *plays a vamp introduction under the following.*

Oleg   Now about this union we are celebrating. I predict it will be a reconciliation of the two classes and all their inherent contradictions, for ever and a day. (*Applause.*)

All   Kiss – kiss!

Oleg   And there's something about this union that we should not forget when we see a twinkle in both the bride and groom's eye. I predict we will soon hear the patter of tiny feet around the beauty salon! Tiny socialist hands raised to be manicured!! What is happening here is the rebirth of family life which over the years has been so damaged by economic savagery of the market place.

All   Shut up you old windbag. Get them to kiss! Kiss! Kiss!

Oleg   Not Marx, not Engels could have dreamed in a thousand years that what we are witnessing could ever take place – Labour and Capital together. What a winning combination! Neither lived to see the heroic class, then obscure, if promising, rise up and seize the reins of history. They never dreamt that in a dramatic development, the conquering hero Labour would take such a shine to Capital – now dethroned but clearly, enduringly alluring. I feel a song coming on.

Oleg *plays on piano.*

(*sings.*)   COME ALL YOU WEDDING GUESTS AND BEAT
YOUR BREASTS ABOUT ME NOW
TO DISPEL THE WICKED RUMOUR THAT THE
BRIDE'S A CUNNING COW

AND TO CAMOUFLAGE THE FACT
THAT SHE IS BOURGEOIS TO HER RUMP
SHE'S HOOKED UP WITH A PROLE
SO THEY CAN HANG ON TO THIS DUMP.

All   WHILE HIS BROTHERS IN THE LITTER
ARE ALL BUTCHERED IN THE YARD
THIS PORKER BY ANOTHER NAME
HOLDS UP HIS UNION CARD
OUR PROLETARIAN HUBBY'S PULLED IT OFF,
THE LITTLE RUNT
FIRST SHE BUFFS HIS PINKY –
NEXT SHE'S STICKING OUT IN FRONT

Usher   Who's that trying to make off with a case of vodka, over there? Come back!

Guest   I was just putting it somewhere safe, honest.

Oleg   Well spotted, Comrade Usher. But no need to bust a blood vessel, just get everyone to relax – (*Calls out.*) Attention please, everyone!

Guests finally fall silent as **Usher** *holds the vodka-thief by the lapels.*

Usher   You're one of those bleeding bourgies, aren't you?

The two sides – hairdressers and mechanics – divide and square up for a fight.

Oleg   People, listen to me! We shouldn't be getting snooty about *occupations*! 'She's a hairdressers and he's mechanic, so they can't get on!' One look at the bride and groom would dispel that nonsense. (*To bride and groom.*) I think that if the hairdressers could all find a mechanic to demonstrate their art on, then both classes will discover exactly why the bride and groom are going to live happily ever after.

A pairing-off of hairdressers and mechanics, mutually suspicious. Tension.

Oleg   THERE'S A CLASS OF PERSONS PRESENT
MALIGNED, MISUNDERSTOOD
WHO IN THIS DAWNING NEW AGE
CAN STILL DO SIMPLE GOOD
I SING IN PRAISE OF HAIRDRESSERS,
ALL AROUND THE WORLD
IT'S AN INTERNATIONAL MOVEMENT,
LET'S HEAR IT FOR THEM, GIRLS –

A squad of hairdressers set upon the rest of the guests and do their hair, against their wishes. A choreographed fight.

Hairdressers   WE LIKE TO CHAT A LITTLE BIT
IT HELPS US PASS THE HOURS
YOU WON'T BELIEVE THE STORIES

> THAT WE HEAR UNDER THE DRIERS
> OH DON'T YOU THINK WE RAISE THE TONE
> AND – WE SHOULD HAVE A UNION OF OUR OWN!

Oleg   NOW HAIRDRESSERS CAN CHANGE
A WOMAN'S THOUGHTS ABOUT HERSELF
THE HAIR DONE RIGHT, SHE'LL NEVER STAY
FOREVER UPON THE SHELF
WHY SHOULD MOTHER NATURE RULE
AND MAKE US ALL UNCHANGED
AND NOW THE REVOLUTION'S COME –
MEN! DON'T BE ASHAMED.

The men fight off the hairdressers. Brawls break out. A stove is knocked over and smoke starts to fill the stage. Smoke increases. The hairdressers are winning, pinning mechanics down in the melée to perm their hair with monstrous combs and spraycans of lacquer, as the stage darkens and pandemonium breaks out.

Hairdressers   ADMITTEDLY, BESIDE THE GOSSIP,
OTHER PASSION PALES
WE FOLLOW FASHION FEARLESSLY
AND DO EACH OTHER'S NAILS
ATTENDING WEDDINGS IS OUR BLISS –
WE'LL GIVE THE BRIDE A LOVING KISS
AND WE DESERVE A UNION OF OUR OWN.

All   (*Various*) Kiss! kiss! /Where's the bride and groom – can't see them – /we're on fire! /Who said fire??? /Fire Brigade – It's out of control! /He-e-elp!)

Blackout.

Scene Four

Firemen *are checking out rows of charred corpses. Enter* **Fire Chief**, *with further group of firemen, officials.*

Chief   What a bloody barbeque, eh? You lot should have rescued at least some of these hapless folk, innocently celebrating what was to have been a happy day.

Fireman 1   It's their own fault. Did anyone bother to call us when the fire started? You drunken bastards! (*Kicks the body bags.*)

Fireman 2   There was nothing we could do, chief. Like, when we arrived, the whole bleeding place was like an oil refinery. Vodka musta been feeding the flames.

Chief   But a hundred percent casualties! It's not going to look good in the records. Dear oh dear. Alright, least said, soonest mended. What have we got here, anyway?

They review the corpses, pulling back the shrouds and dropping them in place again.

Fireman 1   One bod, bonce all spoiled, probably falling beam –

Fireman 3   One charred bod, sex NK, hairdressing tongs in hand, . . .

Fireman 4   One female bod, with wire thingummyjig fried tight on her upper bonce.

Chief   Spare us the details, sonny. I've just had me tea.

Fireman 2 *giving charred notes to* **Fire Chief**.

Fireman 2   One back of the site, criminal and prerevolutionary build, was found with a cash register in his hands.

Fire Chief   (*pockets notes*) Something for the fireman's ball at last. Check the cellar too.

Fireman 2   Can't get down there. It filled up with our water straight off, and froze solid. We did manage to rescue this.

Fire Chief *examines a blackened box, then opens it. It is a case of vodka. Bottles of vodka from the case are handed out to firemen and they line up for their drinking song.*

Chief   Your average standards of safety in this town make Sodom and Gomorrah look like a safe bet. You got to somehow get out there, and educate the people –

(*Sings.*)   TRADITIONAL! – THE MARRIAGE FEAST
WHICH ENDS IN ARMAGEDDON
IT'S QUITE SURPRISING ANYONE
SURVIVES A RUSSIAN WEDDIN',

AND YOU FIREMEN ARE SO LEGLESS
THAT YOU CANNOT POINT A HOSE
PROOF ALCOHOL'S A KILLER,
AVOID THE DREADED DOSE.

Firemen HEAR OUR DREADFUL WARNING, PEOPLE, HEAR
IT LOUD AND CLEAR,
WITH EACH AND EVERY CORK THAT POPS
REHEARSE IT IN YOUR EAR
IF YOU LIKE A DRINK YOU WELL MAY THINK THAT
IT WON'T END IN TEARS,
BUT YOU'RE RISKING FULL COMBUSTION WHEN
YOUR LIVER CHANGES GEAR

OY! OY! THE REDNOSED FIREMEN STRIVE IN VAIN
TO DOUSE THE FLAMES
WE CANNOT GET THE LADDER UP WE CALL EACH
OTHER NAMES
IT'S NEVER TOO LATE TO CELEBRATE – AS THE
FLAMES GO HIGHER
WHAT WAS ONCE A BRIDE AND GROOM
BECOMES A FUNERAL PYRE.

HEAR OUR DREADFUL WARNING, PEOPLE HEAR
IT LOUD AND CLEAR,
WITH EACH AND EVERY CORK THAT POPS
REHEARSE IT IN YOUR EAR (**Firemen** *exiting.*)
OM TIDDLY OM TIDDLY OM, OY! OY!
OM TIDDLY OM TIDDLY OM, OY! OY!
OM TIDDLY OM TIDDLY OM, OY! OY!

Scene Five

Futuristic conference hall with crazy Futurist electronic voting system. An old worker and his apprentice are polishing bits of machinery feebly.

Old Man It's a vital vote, this one today, young shaver. Oil the Agricultural Zones' voting apparatus. We don't want no little mistakes again.

Youth The Central Zones were a bit off as well, and the Smolensk apparatus was coughing a bit.

Old Man Are we forgetting, sonny, that this is a socialist paradise? Everything works, more or less. Just needs a drop of oil. Urals factories are go, Kursk metalworks sections is spanking new with sealed bearings. Runs with 'all the smoothness of a military operation'.

Youth I thought you must remember military operations, Vlad, cos you're so bloody Jurassic and wrinkly.

Old Man I do remember in the old days, just after the revolution, people voting by hand. My mother had to hold me in her arms. And the whole hall was filled with a thousand and one people, and there was all this argy-bargy, and they was split down the middle, exactly on the vote. My mother couldn't vote, of course, she was carrying me in her arms and this stopped her.

Youth That could never happen now.

Old Man Exactly. In the old days, some people stood at the back and pretended they had twelve hands – that can't happen nowadays. (*Enter* **Orator**.) Here comes the president of the Institute for Resurrection. I say! This means an important announcement.

Orator Citizen functionary mechanic and apprentice – Plug in the interactive response registers for all the federation zones! We have an urgent consensus to hold.

Old Man *and* **Youth** *hurry to their places.*

Old Man Yes, suh! Green register go!

Youth Green register on!

Old Man Red register on!

Youth Red register go. All systems go!

Orator Testing testing. One, one, one.

Old Man Test transmission verified, President, transmission commencing forthwith!

Orator   (*coughs. Announcement*) Now hear this! At the corner of 62nd Street and 17th Prospect in the town of Tambov, a building brigade working at a depth of seven metres has unearthed an ice-filled cellar of a previous building. Visible in the midst of the ice is a free-floating, frozen human figure. In the opinion of the Institute for Human Resurrection, this individual, who froze to death very rapidly approximately fifty years ago, could be reactivated. This motion has been circulated by telegram and discussed and we will now proceed to register the different opinions on this proposal. Remember, the Institute for Resurrection considers that the life of every worker must be used until the last possible instant. What we have found is definitely a worker – the hands are calloused, and this is the distinguishing mark of workers around the decade of his entombment. I would remind you that after the wars that swept over the world, and led to the creation of our world federation, human life was declared inviolable by decree. But we should note the objections to resuscitation from members of the Institute of Prevention of Disease, who fear a renaissance of many of the bacillus and bacteria known once to have infested the inhabitants of what was formerly Russia. But remember, comrades, I cannot emphasize this too strongly, we are voting for a human life here!

Lights, bells, buzzers.

In order to further the anthropo-cum-archeological comparative studies into the age in question, the Institute votes for resurrection!

Triumphant music begins. **Orator** *reads message.*

A warning from the sanitary inspection stations in the Don Basin. The hazard to human kind of reviving these archaic bacteria is great, so the sample must remain in a deep frozen state for ever! (*Hubbub.*)
The Siberian agricultural zones request that the defrosting indeed take place, but only after harvest in the autumn so that the Tractorate who have naturally all heard of the monster on their cab radios while harvesting can be witnesses. I can take no more amendments, before voting. All in favour of immediate action raise hands!

A forest of steel hands raise up.

Voting on the Siberian amendement? (*Two hands only.*) The assembly of the Federation hereby accepts the motion for full and immediate resuscitation.

All   Resurrection! Resurrection! Resurrection NOW!

Music swells. Stage floods with reporters who pull old fashioned microphones out of their pockets.

Reporter   – *Eskimo Isvestia?* Clear the front page. It's resurrection! –

Second Reporter   – *Vladivostok Pravda* – newsdesk. Conference have voted for resuscitation – pictures by wire to follow –

Third Reporter – *Berlin and Warsaw Komsol Pravda* – Resurrection confirmed as predicted –

Fourth Reporter – *Chicago Soviet Isvestia* – it's go for resurrection –

Fifth Reporter – *Red Gazette of Rome* – resurrection gets green light –

Sixth Reporter – *Shanghai Weekly Pigeonfancier* – it's go for resurrection –

Seventh Reporter *Los Angeles Weekly Embalmer* – shock horror decision on near-corpse. Ex-guitarist to swear and smoke again.

Newspaper boys bring on papers with headlines saying 'Resurrection'.

Newsboy 1 – Exclusive confessions of neanderthal alcoholic! You'll read it first in the *Red Times of Lagos*! –

Newsboy 2 – In the *Belfast Soviet Weekly Taper* –

Newsboy 3 – Read it in the *Buenos Aires Pravda*-Gleaner

Newsboy 4 – The *All-Red-Buddhist Lhasa Evening Paper*!

The newsboys sing.

Newsboys REARRIVAL OF AN EARLY MAN
THAT DEATH HAD MERCY-KISSED!
YOU NEVER KNOW THE DANGER
AND THE MANY HIDDEN MENACES!
INSTEAD OF KNOWING BETTER
LEAVING WELL ALONE AND AS IT IS –
OUR SCIENTISTS ARE COOKING UP
A MODERN CRYOGENESIS!

They reprise the song as **Zoya**, *much older, comes on and buys a paper, reads the news, and screams. Blackout, end song.*

Scene Six

Zoya *runs in, waving newspaper at* **Professor**, *who is working in cryogenic unit, with frozen iceblock containing* **Varlet**.

Zoya (*panting*) Comrade! Comrade Professor! Don't go through with this! Don't pull the lever or the bleeding shenanigans will start all over again.

Professor Shenanigans . . .? Comrade Byriozka, you appear to have slipped back into the past where I regret to say they spoke an language unknown to today's scientists.

Takes up dictionary.

Zoya Oh, you know what I mean!

Professor I'm afraid to say I don't. Modern life has a very different language, and we have no use for the old words. I don't want to harp on your little mistake though. Slobberchops . . . Shibboleth . . . Here we are. Shenanigans. 'Useless occupation or activity that prevents anything being done.'

Zoya Exactly! Fifty years ago, this 'shenanigans' which you are about to unfreeze caused me to attempt suicide!

Zoya *mimes shooting herself, graphically.*

Professor Suicide? You've got me guessing again. (*Dictionary.*) Suppositious . . . Swabber . . . Suppository. Suspender . . . (*Pause.*) Suicide. (*Reads.*) Oh dear. I suppose they were turbulent times, in those days and there were injustices. Did you try to shoot yourself after receiving a court order from a misguided tribunal, perhaps?

Zoya No. I acted entirely alone.

Professor Then it must have been an accident. It is irrational to end life before it stops being of use to the Party.

Zoya I acted out of disappointed love.

Professor Oh, that is impossible. It is well known that love for the Party means we have children and railway bridges and tractors, and so forth.

Zoya I can't stay if you continue with the reverse cryogenic programme.

Professor But I can't let you go, if you knew it! There is specialized information which we in the Party may need from you to ensure his survival. To survive the trauma of awakening after all these years.

Zoya I think I am going to try and kill myself again.

Professor   I beg you to submerge your personal feelings for the good of the Party.

Zoya   He's going to be hard to bring back. The vodka in his stomach and liver could ignite when you run the defrosting current through him.

Professor *goes to phone.*

Professor   People's fire brigade? Prepare to saturate resuscitation room 451 area with carbon dioxide.

Zoya   What's so wonderful that he's got that needs to be brought back?

Professor   The past, Comrade Byrioska, that obscure country that we carry within ourselves, but so seldom till recently have understood.

Ice block revealed with doctors operating on it as the fire brigade, completely modernized with extinguishers, all arrive at the back, at the double, very brisk and efficient, humming a reprise of the fire-song.

Professor   Switch on the current when I say.

Doctor   Alternating current standing by.

Professor   Now! Bring up the temperature to 98.6 with fifteen-second bursts.

Doctor   Fifteen seconds and counting!

Professor   Have the oxygen ready.

Doctor   Surgical oxygen cylinder and mask ready to go!

Professor   Replace the ice with air pressure as you draw off the melt-water, and I want a full description for the Institute of every physical change he goes through –

Exciting music. Choreographed stenographers taking down the narrative.

Sixth Doctor   Natural colour returning . . . Subject appears almost ice-free . . . Chest movement now perceptible! But some very unusual manual spasms now apparent!

Professor   That's a trapped sensory-reflex from the time he was frozen. Musical, probably: unimportant. They had things which they used to strum with one hand like that, forget what they were called.

Zoya   Oh no, he's coming back with his guitar!

First Doctor   Temperature 98.6

Second Doctor   Pulse is sixty eight per minute.

Sixth Doctor   Breathing regular.

Professor   Stand back, gentlemen! Observe the triumph of science!

Varlet *comes to life, dishevelled. He rises up, clutching his guitar, bending over it, retuning it, croaking along in a broken cracked voice.*

Varlet   (*sings*) THE PARTY WENT OVER THE TOP,
         THEN SOMEONE MUSTA SHOUTED STOP . . .
         (*Twang.*)
         I THINK WE'RE IN A POLICE STATION,
         ME OLD GUITAR! I MUSTA HAVE SLEPT IT OFF
         I'M STARTING TO FEEL ROUGH
         I'D PREFER BY FAR TO BE IN A BAR (*Twang.*)

The firemen surround him and put an end to the song with a burst of dry ice.

Professor   Comrade Neanderthal, this is not a police station.

Varlet *faces* **Professor**.

Varlet   What?

Professor   Drunk tanks are no longer necessary. This is Reverse Cryogenic Room 451 in the Institute for Resurrection where specimens can be thawed out under scientific conditions.

Varlet   Specimens?? I'm a person – I've got documents to prove it! Come off it! You're pissed! You're all pissed! I know doctors – they're never far from the surgical spirit and – it's glug, glug, glug all the time with them . . . what's the date?

Professor   The tenth day of the revolutionary month Blossomy.

Varlet   Not Blossomy, already? I musta been asleep for . . . What year is it then?

Professor   Revolutionary year fifty-nine!

Varlet   You're kidding. Don't tell me it's fifty-nine years . . .

Professor   That's exactly what we are telling you.

Varlet   Oh no! I'd better get the wife a bunch of flowers. She's going to be really pissed off.

Professor   You do not have a wife, specimen.

Varlet   I don't have a wife!!!??? Look, here's my marriage certificate. (*Searches.*) Oh no! Where the bloody hell is it? I can't find it –

Doctor   What's it doing now?

Varlet*'s hands go in and out of pockets faster and faster, trying to find the documents.*

Professor   Dictionary please. We may be able to get a clue from its speech patterns. (*Consults dictionary.*) What you are witnessing, comrades, is a slice of biological history. Deprived of its partner, the male creature is resorting shamelessly to decadent pre-revolutionary self-pleasuring. Extremely unhygienic. Stop it immediately.

Two doctors move forward with a straitjacket and try to put it on **Varlet**.

Varlet Oy! Lemme alone, you wankers!

Professor Dictionary again, please!

Varlet *frees himself from the jacket and throws it down.*

Varlet There's a woman out there, waiting for me – She's been waiting there for fifty years!

Professor The creature is still trapped in fantasy. Comrade Zoya, see if you can obtain the animal's trust, alone.

Zoya *steps forward to be recognized by* **Varlet**. *He stars at her. The rest of the doctors and the* **Professor** *step back.*

Varlet Who's this? Just a minute, don't I know you? –

Lighting change. Music. **Zoya** *and* **Varlet** *approach each other.*

Varlet Blow me down, it's got to be the ex-girlfriend's mother. If not, you're the spitting image – You're not Zoya, are you –

Zoya Yes, I was Zoya. What a fool I was to care about you.

Varlet What they say about it being the future – is true?

Zoya Find out for yourself. You'll never survive in the modern world.

Zoya *throws open a huge door, and traffic noise and fumes pour in and fill the stage.* **Varlet**, *dazzled by the light, peers out into the new world.*

Varlet There's not a horse in sight. Cars, cars, cars! It's inhuman! Where am I? What's going on? Is this Moscow, Paris or New York?

The door closes, and the noise and fumes die away abruptly.

Zoya They should never have unfrozen you.

Varlet That's a cruel thing to say, Zoya. But then you always had a cruel, sarcastic side to you.

Zoya I was the one who was jilted at the altar by you! Remember?

Varlet I don't know what I remember any more. This is all so confusing. Just a moment, here's a little animal friend I recognise! A bedbug! Perhaps you can take me to 17 Lunacharsky Street, little bedbug? Take me back in time again, to where there is singing and dancing, and people there, admittedly drunk, stupid, laughing – but alive.

Zoya You are contemptible!

Varlet   (*sings to bedbug, with guitar*)
LITTLE BED, LITTLE BUG, WHERE YOU GO,
MY HEART GOES WITH YOU,
LITTLE BED LITTLE BUG
SO FAMILIAR TO ME.

The cast come on to take up the refrain en masse, *as the scene changes.*

Cast   LITTLE BED, LITTLE BUG, WHERE YOU GO,
MY HEART GOES WITH YOU,
LITTLE BED LITTLE BUG
SO FAMILIAR TO ME.

Scene Seven

A futuristic city street is revealed with strange trees and futuristic pedestrians. A crowd enters following a reporter.

Reporter Let us refresh ourselves and I will tell you about these grim and terrible events, as we sit under the canopies of the civic omni-arborials.

All take melons and eat them messily.

Man The juice on this here story.

All Spill the beans, watermelon man!!

Reporter You will know that as First Reporter I always have access to the finest class of information – so here it comes!

Points to men hurrying across stage, each with a black bag with a dog's head wearing a stethoscope sticking out of the bag.

Reporter There are three epidemics now raging in the town. See that? Those men are vets – The epidemic started when the resurrected early mammal made contact with some of our advanced domestic animals – and now the dogs don't bark any more, they don't play, they only go around on their hind legs, smirking, winking and generally ingratiating themselves to diners in restaurants, and then – they bite. The doctors say that anyone who is bitten by one of these animals will develop all the symptoms of infection before going on to bite someone else.

All Disgusting! Outrageous!

Reporter Now look at this! Disease number two!

*A **Fireman** rolls by, drunk.*

Fireman WALK BACKWARDS WITH ME TO THE GOOD OLD
DAYS
YOU COULD GET LEGLESS IN SO MANY WAYS
– ALL THE DIFFERENT POSITIONS
– FUN WITH VOMITING COMPETITIONS
THE LIVER ON FIRE
ONLY LEADING WHERE THE HEART DESIRES
YOU COULD RELAX EVERY SPHINCTER
FLOWING HAPPY AND FREE –
IN THE GOOD OL' NINETEENTH CENTURY

Reporter See that? He's done for as well! There are already one hundred and seventy five workers infected just like him.

Several firemen take up the tune and hum softly as they weave backwards and forwards, all over the stage.

Reporter   They say this one may be even more contagious.

Man   This is dreadful! How on earth did it start?

Reporter   To revive the unfrozen early mammal, a fermented mixture you may have heard of was used, called 'beer'. During the preparation great care was taken but some has been ingested. Five-hundred-and-twenty workers have been hospitalized and the numbers are growing every day!

Man   As an historian, I know about this 'beer'. I predict the mysterious illness can only be conquered if enough volunteers come forward – and for the good of the people, I will put myself forward immediately as a test case to be inoculated!

Applause from the crowd. Bows and exits.

Music, guitar. Enter girl, dancing by herself.

Reporter   The third aspect of the plague. Any women who live within earshot of the crazed, infected mammal, hear him at night, when the town is silent, hear the plunk of his horny plectrum on his depraved instrument through the thin walls – finally this noise becomes too much for our girls – they go out of their minds –

Man   This I do not believe! How can this be?

Reporter   Infection rates of 'Lurve' as it is known, are running at over seventy-five percent of all within earshot!

All   'Lurve' microbes are poisoning every cubic centimetre of our air!

The single girl is joined by several others, inhaling imaginary roses and swooning about the stage, they swoop around, to music, humming in a trance.

Reporter   At a certain stage, 'Lurve' victims repond to a further set of stimuli. They come together on a hidden signal, and somehow the parasitic infection synchronizes all infected legs, in a low parody of decadent bourgeois art!

Suddenly the girls come together to do high kicks, in an intense, professional looking, insect-like conga.

Man   (*amazed*) How on earth is that done??

Reporter   We don't know yet, but the epidemic is reaching crisis proportions! It's as if some sort of depraved primitive consciousness is taking over the world!

*Enter **Director**, with a magnifying glass. The girls keep dancing in conga round him.*

Director   Attention, please! A search-party has reported that the precious final example of the unique bloodsucking creature, the klop, or bedbug, has been sighted here a quarter of an hour ago, heading for the fourth floor, average speed one and a half miles per hour – Comrades – search the premises, immediately!

Everyone searches while the girls dance through them.

Reporter   You'll never find it this way. The only way to capture a bedbug is to lay out some bait –

Voice   Put a naked man on a mattress in every window!

Voices   Don't shout, you'll frighten it away!

Director   Anyone who finds it is warned not to try to secrete it about their person. This bedbug is state property and a severe fine will be levied if it is found on any person!

Voice   Here it is! Here it is!

Spotlight on one spot on stage. The girls stop dancing.

Director   Yes that's it! Firemen, over here!

Charade with drunken firemen, trying to trap it in helmet, and ladders.

Director   It's over here now! Bastard got away! Never fear, quick –

Fireman   Got it!

Director   Don't let it fall – it'll kill itself! Do not crush the insect's legs! Careful!!

Voices   Got it, hurrah!

Director   Careful, now – the capture, using the highest technology in a previously undreamed of combination, has been resoundingly successful. Now you be quiet, folks, please. It has crossed its legs and wishes to rest! Thank you, Comrades, for your struggles which will, I'm, sure, further our scientific knowledge. This is an unique specimen of *Bedbugus normalis*, extremely popular at the beginning of the revolutionary era and believed extinct subsequently. Now our city zoological gardens will be the first to exhibit it, and if we're not on the tourist map after this, I'll eat my tricycle. I invite all present, including gentlemen of the press to a formal inauguration of *Bedbugus normalis*'s new life in captivity.

Exit all, to important dead march music, carrying the bedbug ceremonially off on a velvet cushion.

Scene Eight

Cryogenic ward. **Varlet** *strums on his guitar, melancholy.*

Varlet Professor, c'm'ere – gimme some hair of the dog, will you?

Doctor *gives beer, a small amount.*

Varlet This amount hasn't got a snowball in hell's chance of curing a hangover. What about a litre and a half of vodka, then?

Professor I could not be responsible for giving you a lethal dose.

Varlet Did I ask to be resurrected? Freeze me back! (*Slurred.*) What 'smatter? Scared?

Professor We are not empowered to act separately from the collective, and the life of each worker is sacred.

Varlet But your charter doesn't include me. I mean, I'm not working here, am I? So what is sacred about me now? Gimme a proper drink.

Enter **Zoya** *with books.*

Zoya I've got the books for you. I don't know whether they are what you want. Nowhere carries books in praise of 'Lurve'. Or roses, or daydreams, the closest I could get was a textbook on horticulture.

Varlet This is why I would rather die. Emotion – do any of you know what that is? What did we fight for in the old days? We fought because we wanted to dance and sing and be happy. What happened?

Doctor We have dancing in our modern state. Tomorrow, twenty-thousand male and female workers will celebrate the collective harvest with a dance around a thousand-tractor rally in the people's arena.

Takes paper sandwiched between books.

Varlet Aw, I can't wait. Look you don't want me here. Even I can see that. Give me what I want or pop me back in the permafrost. (*Pause.*)

Professor (*to* **Zoya**) There is a sort of subhuman logic to what he is saying. We just don't have the resources to provide what he wants.

Zoya I'd deep-freeze him again without a second's regret, if it was my decision.

Varlet *has found a flyer in the books that* **Zoya** *brought in.*

Varlet Zoya – explain – please – what's this bumf about?

Zoya It's just a jobsheet. They give them out free on the streets.

Varlet   It says 'Human being wanted'? Human being! That's me. None of you are qualified.

Zoya   The city is committed to full employment, and I must have picked one up . . .

Varlet   'Ordinary human being wanted! Job at civic zoo' See – Someone wants me!

Professor   Are you sure?

Professor *goes to phone.*

Varlet   I could do this! I could do this job!

Professor   (*into phone*) Zoo Director? This is the Institute for Resurrection. We think we may have a candidate who would fit your advertisement. Of course, we shall be sad to see him go . . .

Scene Nine

The stage fills with animals. Zoo with elephants, giraffes, and musicians and stewards directing people to grandstands. A cage draped with cloth, centre. The band plays.

Steward This way, foreign Comrade-journalists! Next to the platform, leave room for the Brazilians – their airship is landing at this moment in the central airport. Sun-blessed Comrades, kindly mix in with the climatically-challenged British visitors, that way we can get a memorable and striking effect. Oh, it looks a picture. You high-school students, over to the left, listen up. Four veterans from the Union of Centenarians have elected to supplement the professor's lecture with thrilling eyewitness examples of the old time, fresh-culled from their memory banks.

Happy old people come forward in a dense clanking phalanx of Zimmer frames.

Old Man Oh now! – I remember it like it was now.

Old Woman No, it's me who remembers it like it was now!

Second Old Man You remember like it was now, but I can remember what it was like *before* now.

Old Woman Oh I can remember before that, before *before* now. I can remember a *very* long time ago.

Old Man Oh I remember that time, but also what it was like before that! All of which I remember like it was yesterday! What day is it today?

Steward Thank you, veterans! Right now we've got the distilled experience of beardless Youth to hear – by the right, quick march!

Children enter marching.

Children WE'RE PRODIGIES, WE'RE ALL AT EASE,
ALGEBRA AND MATHS WE KNOW IT ALL.
TO MAKE A CHANGE FROM SQUARING ROOTS
WE'RE OFF TO IRRITATE THE MARMOSETS AND
STOATS
AND THEN WE'LL POKE THE FRISKY LITTLE GOATS,
AND JUST FOR LAUGHS
UPSET GIRAFFES

Steward Take these now, children.

Girl Cor, what are these?

Boy And what's this disgusting-smelling slop?

Steward   Now children, can you guess which animal likes the things you're holding?

Girl   An ostrobogulous! (*Titters, shushed.*)

Steward   These are animal nutrition units, products specifically created by the Central Medical Institute for one special creature. And follow my instructions to the letter, or it may be the worse for you!

Steward *handing out drinks and cigarettes.*

Steward   Your school has been chosen to feed the latest acquisition.

(*Sings.*)   YOU'VE GOT TO HAVE A CARE
WHEN YOU'RE OFFERING A BEAR
AN APPLE OR TINY HUNK OF FISH
THE BEAR WILL BE AWARE THAT LIFE IS SO UNFAIR
NOT AS MUCH IS NOW ON OFFER AS IT – MIGHT –
WISH

Schoolkids   THOSE WHO ENTER LION'S CAGES
ALL DESERVE DOUBLE WAGES,
HIPPOPOTAMUSES OFT CHARGE QUITE
UNPROVOKED.
WE SHOULD BEWARE THE CALL
OF THAT MYSTERIOUS ANIMAL
A DRINKER, WHO LIKES TO SMOKE.

FEED THE ANIMAL WHAT IT ADORES
THEN MARVEL AT ITS SWEATY PORES.

GETTING THE ANIMAL DRUNK, WOO WOO
DRUNK AS A COUPLE OF SKUNKS
GETTING THE ANIMAL LEGLESS
GETTING THE ANIMAL DRUNK

GETTING THE ANIMAL DRUNK
GETTING THE ANIMAL DRUNK
SWEARING AND SPITTING AND FIGHTING AND
SQUITTING
GETTING THE ANIMAL DRUNK

Steward   And now – please greet the chairman and committee of the City Soviet!

Enter **Chairman. Committee** *sing.*

Committee   WE SEND FRATERNAL GREETINGS TO THE
WORKERS OF THE ZOO
WE SOVIET CITY WORKERS ALL APPLAUD
WHAT YOU DO,
HEROES OF LABOUR

WITH RHINOS FOR NEIGHBOURS!
HURRAH! THE SPINY PORCUPINE WILL,
WITH ITS LITTLE MOTTLED QUILL –
DO AND DO AND DO
WE SEND FRATERNAL GREETINGS TO
THE WORKERS OF THE ZOO

Chairman   Comrades, children, other species. Since external mishaps have been minimized in our modern society, there is time now for us to develop interest in spectacle, that however extravagant it may be in appearances, contains significant scientific and historic truths. We can spend hours staring at the multicoloured and inflamed posterior of baboons, and we can link the sight with a deeper understanding of the past struggles of the world proletariat.

I'd say the latest arrival was easily as entertaining as any of the droll creatures we have here already. Mr Zoo Director, we applaud you, and I hand over the chair.

Applause, music fanfare. **Director** *goes up to podium.*

Director   If it had not been for the kind offer of my colleague the professor at the Institute of Resurrection, these – two – specimens of a bygone era would not be available for our edification tonight. Initially, we were only aware of one. We first caught *Bedbugus normalis*, it was on its own, but we knew we would need a *Homo sapiens* feedsource to keep the specimen alive. But how? We have evolved far beyond them. I put out an advertisement, and to my astonishment a mammalian specimen was made available. When the specimen arrived at the Zoo, we discovered that it was *Bourgeoisus vulgaris*, not noble *Homo sapiens*. However *Bedbugus normalis* is not too choosy, thankfully, and both have settled into their little routine quite happily. *Bourgeoisus vulgaris*, in the era this specimen is from, affected horrid passions for what was called 'culture'. It was not possible to avoid *Bourgeoisus*'s cultural droppings filling the insteps of your shoes, wherever you stepped.

Keepers sweep round **Varlet***'s draped cage, carefully.*

In the past, it was disgusting and contagious but today we have a system which continuously removes any culture that the animal deposits so you are all quite safe. Comrades and Comradesses, *Bedbugus normalis* and *Bourgeoisus vulgaris* in an exact replica of their natural habitat. Behold!

Curtains fall away to show **Varlet** *on a bed with a bottle, and guitar. Crowd approach.* **Varlet** *plucks guitar listlessly.* **Director** *steps into the cage, puts on rubber gloves, draws gun, and turns a listless* **Varlet** *round for the zoo visitors.*

Director   Come closer, comrades, don't be frightened. It's quite tame. Look, this is something you won't have seen before. It's going to have a 'smoke'.

Voice   Is that what those tubes are for? Disgusting!

Director   And it's going to have some 'booze'.

Voice   This is cruel – watching animals take poison! We shouldn't be tormenting it!

Director   Would you like to come for a little walkies, *Bourgeiosus*? Come on! See, it knows its name. Come on, leave your little chum under the bed and come for walkies. He just dropped a whole lot of culture before you arrived – he generally only does that once a day. So it's comletely safe . . .

Director *opens the cage door and retreats. Slowly* **Varlet** *comes out and peers around.*

Director   Say 'hello' to the nice people.

Director *slowly backs away from* **Varlet**, *who looks at the crowd disinterested, then turns back to the theatre audience, and starts to peer at them excited for the first time. Recognition. The speech starts with a whisper and ends up shouting.*

Varlet   Hey – just a minute – citizens! Hundreds of them. Brothers! My own, my very own people! People like me! How did you get in here? So many of you? When were you all unfrozen? Oh, this is marvellous – but why am I kept all alone in the cage when there are so many of you? We could have a party. Come and join me please immediately! All of you! (*Yells.*) I'm so lonely – It hurts to be alone. So alone!

Director   Get the children out of here – they shouldn't be hearing this!

Varlet *sinks to his knees. Children scream. Crowd panic.*

Varlet   I'm sad, so sad, sad, sad. Life has cheated me . . . Join me . . . Why am I suffering like this?

Children scream again.

Varlet   Touch me. Come closer! (*Sobs.*)

Two attendants grab **Varlet** *and throw him back in the cage.*

Director   Apologies for what you heard, comrades. The bright lights must have caused it to hallucinate. Please remain calm. There's no one out there. The specimen display is concluded now. Band! Let's give the citizens a merry marching song as they disperse to their neat homes.

We see **Varlet** *start to pick out the first tune he played on the guitar, sadly, on his own as the crowd disperses. Fade lights.*

The Grotesque Proletarian and Promenade Revolutionary

Snoo Wilson interviewed by Jim Mulligan

In the late sixties, the University of East Anglia was the place to be for those who would become writers. Snoo Wilson went there to work with luminaries such as Angus Wilson, Malcolm Bradbury, Jonathan Raban and Victor Sage. He submitted plays as part of his coursework and has had a steady stream of successes since 1970. In 25 years he has been Associate Director of Portable Theatre, Script Editor for the BBC's *Play for Today*, and Dramaturg for the Royal Shakespeare Company. He has taught film scriptwriting at the National Film School, worked at Santa Cruz University and the New York Theatre Studio, and was Associate Professor lecturing in playwriting at University College, San Diego.

'I had been interested in Mayakovsky for a long time, so when the National asked me to adapt *The Bedbug*, it was a gift. Politically, Mayakovsky was ambiguous. He saw himself as a poet of the people, a son of Russia, a revolutionary who rose through the masses. On the other hand, he wasn't quite as idealistic as Gorky, another great Russian survivor, nor was he outside the system like Venedict Erofeyev, the nearest thing to a Beat Poet that Russia produced. Mayakovsky was a manic-depressive, who killed himself in 1929 when it was clear that the authorities were going to get him. But in that first tempestuous decade of the Revolution, he wrote plays such as *The Bedbug* and poems in praise of Stalin as other writers were being sent off to Siberia. It is always difficult for authorities to deal with satire.'

What comes through, fifty years after *The Bedbug* was written, is a bawdy humour and a distrust of authority. Snoo Wilson sees a significant part of Mayakovsky in the character of Ivan.

'Mayakovsky started life as a working-class revolutionary and became a performer, a dandy who liked the high life, a promenade revolutionary who went to Paris and considered himself a cosmopolitan. Ivan, the grotesque proletarian and grasping survive-at-all-costs plebeian is, in part at least, a self portrait. It would have been politically and dramatically apt if Ivan had woken, after fifty years, in the Brezhnev era, so that we could have seen the irony of what Oleg says: "Labour and Capital together. What a winning combination!" But the play wasn't written like that. My play is not a literal translation. That is what I started from and then I adapted it. I tried to be true to the nature of the original, which is written as seven panels of action, with songs like inverted commas round each action.'

Music by Shostakovich was used in the original, but Snoo Wilson has left individual companies to find their own way of integrating the music into the dramatic production. One of the problems of the play is that, up to the fire, it is all farce in a gritty, realistic and recognisable setting, and then there is repentance in an antiseptic brave new world, where everything has been sanitised and controlled. 'Although the play ends in a fantasy world, it is dealing with the death of idealism and the realisation that you have to deal with the tacky reality of humanity as well as its aspirations. We don't know what kind of a world those early revolutionaries dreamed of, but it surely can't have been the one Mayakovsky presents. He must have had his tongue in his cheek. But the microbes Ivan releases into this perfect world are the very ones that destroyed the Revolution. The dogs on their hind legs, who bite people and infect them, are the sycophants. The drunkenness and the hangover that follow are part of the Russian temperament. The third microbe, "Lurve", is a reflection on the early attempts of the Revolution to subjugate human relationships to the common good.'

The Bedbug is more than a commentary on a political system. After the First World War, the theatre, art, cinema, literature, and practically every aspect of creative life were influenced by the Futurists. They had a vision of progress which influenced style; Mayakovsky was perceived as an artist with an individual voice and, therefore, a threat to the socialist system which he was supposed to be celebrating. The play is a fairy-tale where someone falls asleep and wakes up in a different world though with the same sensibilities. But the treatment Mayakovsky gives the story is different from anything that was being done in the English theatre. The fact that his style is now commonplace is a tribute to his influence.

'You look in vain to find anyone in the 1920s and '30s who is doing the same as Mayakovsky. The anarchy and humour are most like Alfred Jarry's famous *Ubu* plays. Ivan, like Ubu, is a huge part which carries its own contradictions. I don't see why young people should not relate this play to our contemporary situation. After all, the things Mayakovsky is laughing at are greed, vanity, and believing that you are better than you are because you have money and social position. These things have moral dimensions that transcend any particular society. There are more than enough examples of that corruption of the spirit in our own society for young people to ponder on.'

Snoo Wilson is a distinguished playwright with a long list of plays to his name, including *Vampire*, *The Number of the Beast*, *Pignight*, *More Light*, and most recently *Darwin's Flood* and *HRH*. His work has been produced by the Royal Shakespeare Company, and at the Royal Court, the Bush and throughout the United States. He has also written films, librettos and radio plays – including two scripts about Dr Johnson, played by Simon Callow, for the BBC. He adapted Venedict Erofeyev's *Walpurgis Night* for the Gate Theatre, London, and his most recent plays in London were *More Light* and *Darwin's Flood* at the Bush Theatre. His writing has been described as 'a fantastic toyshop whose timeless contraptions – genuine luxury goods from all the ages – whirr, fizz and explode in their collisions as if by magic.'

The Bedbug

Production Notes

Setting and staging

The play moves at a fast pace and is wild and outrageous. The first section, before the fire, needs to contrast sharply with the post-decadent, futuristic world which follows. The following **settings** need to be suggested: a street; a grotty hostel with dirty bunks; a beauty parlour where a stove starts the fire; and – fifty years on – a futuristic conference hall; a laboratory cryogenic world; a futuristic street scene; and a zoo.

Music will have to be composed to accompany the lyrics.

Special effects include fire, smoke, dry-ice, and traffic fumes. (Ivan is contained in an ice block at one point). The bedbug might be real or imagined.

Sound effects include a foxtrot from a crackling gramophone; noisy traffic; and gunshot.

The chorus become in turn a crowd, hairdressers, firemen (later doubling as doctors), charred corpses, reporters, futuristic pedestrians, animals, children, men with dogs' heads, students, and happy old people with Zimmer frames. The chorus will greatly help to suggest the various settings. The hairdressers might, for instance, work with larger-than-life combs or scissors. The reporters could hold extra-large, old fashioned microphones. These visual images need to be immediate and obvious, and therefore quick-change **costumes** are essential. With regard to costumes, it is worth considering the use of rich and varied colours in the first half, and more neutral shades for the futuristic setting.

Casting

The play requires a cast of at least twenty, with singing ability, plus a band. As well as the Chorus, there are Ivan; Elzevir; her mother Rosalie; her father David; Zoya (a working girl who has aged fifty years by the second section); a professor; a zoo director; and an orator. A large amount of 'doubling up' is possible, and the band should be very much part of the action.

Questions

1. To what extent is *The Bedbug* a deeply pessimistic appraisal of the Communist Revolution?

2. What aspect of Russian life does the play disparage?

3. The play can be described as a timeless fairy-story wherein someone falls asleep and wakes up in a different world. What other tales carry a similar theme?

4. To what extent does Ivan represent 'Everyman' and the baseness of human nature?

5. Can *The Bedbug* be described as 'a political play'? How could it be developed to reflect more closely the current political situation in Russia?

Exercises

1. Improvise the scene in the cryogenic unit when Ivan is revived. Discover what effect he would have on the play if he awoke in a positive spirit, happy to be alive fifty years on.

2. In groups, rapidly create a series of 'freeze-frames' to depict the hairdressers, the firemen, the futuristic pedestrians, the animals. Break the 'freeze-frames' by adding action. Decide what distinct movements can successfully be used to differentiate between the various groups of characters. Introduce hand-held props, e.g. large combs for the hairdressers, tangled hoses and bottles of vodka for the firemen. As a group, experiment with props and make them part of the action. The object is to define clearly the identity of each group with the minimum of accessories – through different forms of movement, for example.

3. 'Hot-seat' Zoya and ask her to describe events that have happened in the intervening years between the first and second sections of the play.

4. Take the characters in the wedding scene and decide what status they have, the highest being 10 and the lowest 2. Put them in a line, illustrating the descending status – highest at the front and lowest at the back. The actors then pass an instruction down the line, in character, from one person to the next, and then have them pass the same instruction back to the front, maintaining individual status throughout. Concentrating on Ivan and Zoya, decide how their status is affected by events in the play. Select a scene where the status of either one of them is challenged. Decide how differing social status can be affected on stage.

Suzy Graham-Adriani
Director/Producer for BT National Connections

Methuen Student Editions

John Arden	*Serjeant Musgrave's Dance*
Alan Ayckbourn	*Confusions*
Aphra Behn	*The Rover*
Edward Bond	*Lear*
Bertolt Brecht	*The Caucasian Chalk Circle*
	Life of Galileo
	Mother Courage and her Children
Caryl Churchill	*Top Girls*
Shelagh Delaney	*A Taste of Honey*
John Galsworthy	*Strife*
Robert Holman	*Across Oka*
Henrik Ibsen	*A Doll's House*
Charlotte Keatley	*My Mother Said I Never Should*
John Marston	*The Malcontent*
August Strindberg	*The Father*
J. M. Synge	*The Playboy of the Western World*
Oscar Wilde	*The Importance of Being Earnest*
Tennessee Williams	*A Streetcar Named Desire*

Methuen Modern Plays

include work by

Jean Anouilh

John Arden

Margaretta D'Arcy

Peter Barnes

Brendan Behan

Edward Bond

Bertolt Brecht

Howard Brenton

Simon Burke

Jim Cartwright

Caryl Churchill

Noël Coward

Sarah Daniels

Nick Dear

Shelagh Delaney

David Edgar

Dario Fo

Michael Frayn

John Guare

Peter Handke

Jonathan Harvey

Declan Hughes

Terry Johnson

Barrie Keeffe

Stephen Lowe

Doug Lucie

John McGrath

David Mamet

Arthur Miller

Mtwa, Ngema & Simon

Tom Murphy

Peter Nichols

Joe Orton

Louise Page

Luigi Pirandello

Stephen Poliakoff

Franca Rame

David Rudkin

Willy Russell

Jean-Paul Sartre

Sam Shepard

Wole Soyinka

Theatre Workshop

Sue Townsend

Timberlake Wertenbaker

Victoria Wood

Methuen World Classics

Aeschylus (two volumes)
Jean Anouilh
John Arden (two volumes)
Arden & D'Arcy
Aristophanes (two volumes)
Aristophanes & Menander
Peter Barnes (two volumes)
Brendan Behan
Aphra Behn
Edward Bond (four volumes)
Bertolt Brecht
  (four volumes)
Howard Brenton
  (two volumes)
Büchner
Bulgakov
Calderón
Anton Chekhov
Caryl Churchill
  (two volumes)
Noël Coward (five volumes)
Sarah Daniels (two volumes)
Eduardo De Filippo
David Edgar (three volumes)
Euripides (three volumes)
Dario Fo (two volumes)
Michael Frayn (two volumes)
Max Frisch
Gorky
Harley Granville Barker
  (two volumes)
Henrik Ibsen (six volumes)

Lorca (three volumes)
David Mamet
Marivaux
Mustapha Matura
David Mercer
  (two volumes)
Arthur Miller
  (four volumes)
Anthony Minghella
Molière
Tom Murphy
  (three volumes)
Peter Nichols
  (two volumes)
Clifford Odets
Joe Orton
Louise Page
A. W. Pinero
Luigi Pirandello
Stephen Poliakoff
  (two volumes)
Terence Rattigan
Ntozake Shange
Sophocles (two volumes)
Wole Soyinka
David Storey (two volumes)
August Strindberg
  (three volumes)
J. M. Synge
Ramón del Valle-Inclán
Frank Wedekind
Oscar Wilde

Methuen New Theatrescripts

include work by

April de Angelis
Iraj Jannatie Ataie
Harwant Bains
Sebastian Barry
Simone de Beauvoir/
   Diana Quick
Paul Boakye
Richard Cameron
Fred D'Aguiar
Rod Dungate
Marieluise Fleisser/
   Tinch Minter
Nikolai Gogol/Adrian Mitchell
Bonnie Greer
Noël Greig
Jonathan Harvey
Robert Holman
Kevin Hood
Karen Hope
Declan Hughes
Tunde Ikoli

Elfriede Jelinek/Tinch Minter
Judith Johnson
Manfred Karge/Tinch Minter &
   Anthony Vivis
Barrie Keeffe
Thomas Kilroy
Maureen Lawrence
Claire Luckham
Anthony Minghella
Phyllis Nagy
Winsome Pinnock
Joe Pintauro
Philip Ridley
Rob Ritchie
Diane Samuels
David Spencer
Edward Thomas
Michael Wilcox
Nicholas Wright
Rod Wooden
Sheila Yeger

Methuen Young Drama

Richard Cameron	*Strugglers*
F. K. Waechter/Ken Campbell	*Clown Plays*
Ken Campbell	*Skungpoomery*
David Holman	*Whale*
George Orwell/Peter Hall	*Animal Farm*
Willy Russell	*Our Day Out*
Sue Townsend	*The Secret Diary of Adrian Mole aged 13¾: The Play*

Methuen Audition Books and Monologues

Annika Bluhm (ed)   *The Methuen Audition Book for Men*
The Methuen Audition Book for Women

Michael Earley and
Philippa Keil (eds)   *The Classical Monologue – Men*
The Classical Monologue – Women
The Contemporary Monologue – Men
The Contemporary Monologue – Women
The Modern Monologue – Men
The Modern Monologue – Women

Anne Harvey (ed)   *The Methuen Audition Book for Young Actors*
The Methuen Book of Duologues for Young Actors